To Hell in a Handbasket

Ruthie Blum

TO HELL IN A HANDBASKET

Carter, Obama,
and the "Arab Spring"

RVP Press
New York

RVP Publishers Inc.
95 Morton Street, Ground Floor
New York, NY 10014

RVP Press, New York

Photo cover: iStockphoto
Photo author: Ariel Jerozolimski

RVP Press™ is an imprint of RVP Publishers Inc., New York
The RVP Publishers logo is a registered trademark of RVP Publishers Inc., New York

Library of Congress Control Number: 2012942847

ISBN 978 1 61861 333 2

www.rvppress.com

To my mother and father, Midge Decter and Norman Podhoretz, who taught me how to speak my truth—and who have always been there to pick up the pieces when my doing so has curried no favor.

Table of Contents

Foreword

BY DAVID AZRIELI

In 1990, I took two of my grown daughters with me to Poland. The purpose of the trip was to retrace the literal and figurative journey I had made from my home town of Makow in 1939 to my homeland of (pre-state) Israel three years later.

I had spent the better part of adulthood dissociating myself from that chapter of my past. I had wanted nothing to do with the country where I was born and raised by loving parents who met their fate in the ovens of Auschwitz and Birkenau. The adolescence I spent escaping Nazi capture had felt like a Pandora's Box better left shut.

The time had come to open it, and to let my children finally receive more than the disjointed morsels I had grudgingly given them over the years in response to their probing questions.

By now, I had become a successful architect, businessman and philanthropist, dividing my time between my homes in Israel and Canada. Returning to Poland, then, was not only my way of getting closure after the horrors of World War II. It was also an assertion of victory over the Nazis and their atrocities—a tribute to how far I had come since then; and how fortunate I was not only to have survived, but to have flourished and been blessed with a beautiful, vibrant family, free of the fetters and perils of anti-Semitism. Thus far, at least.

Starting out in Warsaw, my daughters and I followed the path I had been forced to take as a 17-year-old Jewish boy fleeing for his life and heading for Palestine. From there we proceeded on to Makow, moving from town to town. We even made our way to the Soviet Union.

The one place we could not visit was the last leg of my flight to freedom: Iran. Just over a decade earlier, the country had been overtaken by the radical Ayatollah Khomeini and his followers, making it impossible for Canadian Jews like us to enter. As a result, our excursion ended in Stalingrad, where Perestroika was in full swing.

No such reform movement was taking place in the Islamic Republic, however. On the contrary, the reign of terror and tyranny that had replaced the pro-Western regime of the Shah eleven years earlier was in full swing. That this former ally of North America and Israel remains a mullah stronghold to this day—with a president hell bent not only on acquiring nuclear weapons, but vowing to use them against Israel—is the impetus for this book, which I hope will serve as a cautionary tale.

The world that defeated Nazism and Communism is now under a threat no less demonic—that of global jihad. It is a threat that should have been nipped in the bud when it began to rear its ugly head in the mid-1970s. But that would have required the administration in Washington to be prepared to recognize and fight against it, rather than first dismiss and then appease it. Imagine the consequences had American leaders responded similarly when confronted with Hitler and Stalin. Imagine the outcome had Jimmy Carter been the leader of the Free World during the Third Reich.

Three stops my daughters and I made that had not been part of my original travels were the death camps of Treblinka, Auschwitz and Birkenau. I needed to show them—and see for myself—the places where millions of Jews had been slaughtered, my family among them. I wanted, too, to overcome my ambivalence about reciting the Kaddish, the Jewish mourners' prayer, at those ghoulish "tourist" sites where the remains of my parents and siblings lay.

At Auschwitz, past the gates with the *Arbeit Macht Frei* (work sets you free) sign overhead, we encountered a group of Native Americans on a tour of the bunkers where all the belongings of Jews who had been gassed to death and then cremated are on display: mountains of hair, shoes, spectacles—room after room of Nazi collections, all kept, all categorized. It seemed oddly touching that these non-Jews with no connection to the Holocaust should be taking part in this particular commemoration.

We ran into them again at Birkenau, walking distance away. Here they sat, chanting and beating a drum, their own prayer for the dead. I was overcome with emotion, overwhelmed by the thread tying to such seemingly unrelated people at this historically significant place—the thread of a shared acknowledgement and denunciation of evil; the common assertion of the triumph of good.

Still, standing here nearly five decades after these camps had been liberated by Allied forces, I was painfully aware that the Free World in general, and Israel in particular, might be no less in jeopardy than Europe had been in when I was a child, blissfully untouched by the imminent horrors that were soon to befall.

By this point, in 1990, Israelis were experiencing the malevolent effects of terrorism on a regular basis. Indeed, Yasser Arafat's Palestinian Liberation Organization and other Arab groups made no secret of their plans to destroy the Jewish State.

Yet it was during this very year that ex-president Jimmy Carter was becoming fast friends with the PLO chief, not only meeting with him, but helping write his speeches for Western ears.

Instead of being discredited for this, however, Carter was and continues to be praised by the Left for serving as a self-appointed, free-floating "human rights" diplomat, negotiating with despots across the globe, winning awards and raising large sums from dubious sources for the Carter Center he created in 1982.

He has also been writing best-selling books. The most notorious of these, *Palestine: Peace Not Apartheid*, is filled with such blatant lies about Israel that it caused long-time Carter Center director Kenneth Stein to resign in protest. When this shameful work was published in 2006, Israelis were still stinging from the Second Lebanon War, instigated by Hizbullah; years of suicide attacks against innocent civilians inside its borders; incessant Hamas rocket fire from a by then *judenrein* Gaza Strip; and from the abduction of a number of IDF soldiers, most notably Corporal Gilad Schalit (whose release on October 18, 2011—after five years in captivity—cost Israel, in turn, the release of 1,027 Palestinian terrorists from its jails.)

All of the above was carried out with the financial and military backing of the regime in Tehran, now led by Mahmoud Ahmadinejad, who had come to power the year before. This was the very same Ahmadinejad who was vowing to wipe Israel off the map—the very same Ahmadinejad who was among the Iranian students who had seized the US Embassy in Tehran in 1979, holding dozens of Americans hostage for 444 days. And while these 52 US foreign-service people were imprisoned, interrogated and abused, President Carter tried to negotiate their release through middlemen. By the time he finally gave the green light to a rescue operation, it was too little, too late. The operation failed miserably, leaving in its wake eight dead American servicemen, much to the delight of the hostage-takers and their mentor, Khomeini. What better proof, as far as they were concerned, that Allah was on their side, helping them achieve their ultimate goal of world dominance through Islam?

I felt angry at the attention the Carter book was receiving. I was bowled over by the mendacity of this respected "elder," who was unabashedly continuing to assist Israel's enemies by giving their knowingly false claims legitimacy. Outrageous doesn't begin to describe the gall of this man and his admirers. Not only were his policies as president responsible for the loss of Iran to the ayatollahs in the first place; his behavior since then—as an appeaser of any and all world leaders and groups antithetical to the values he supposedly holds so dear—suggests that he is either a fool or an ideologue of the sort who would have the worst of history repeat itself. Perhaps he is a bit of both.

I began to feel the need to connect the dots between Carter and the current global crisis, particularly since President Barack Obama seems to be following a similar path.

It was then that I considered the possibility of having a book written on the subject.

I was familiar with Ruthie Blum through her weekly articles in The Jerusalem Post. I first met her when she came to interview me for the paper in 2008. Not a stranger to journalists by any means, I was nevertheless impressed with how well she was able to grasp and convey my words.

About a year later, I was struck by a column she wrote describing her own trip to Poland to see the death camps. Within months, she and I were discussing a collaboration to reveal Carter's culpability in the rise and spread of political Islam—through the story of his handling of the hostage crisis.

Much has been said and written about the former one-term president, some of it, of course, critical. But though his failures should have made him an irrelevant "has-been," he and his worldview are alive and well in the Obama administration—if anything, even more dangerously so.

Indeed, as Iran sails in what looks like a smooth journey to acquiring nuclear bombs, the rest of the Muslim world has been emboldened by Obama to become ever more radicalized. Proof of this lies in the behavior both of the Middle Eastern countries engaged in the so-called "Arab Spring," and in Obama's response to it. Just as Carter helped the rise to power of the mullah-led regime in Tehran, so is Obama handing the rest of the region to the anti-Western Islamists on a silver platter.

Mourning at Auschwitz was something I needed to do to come to terms with a tragic past. The purpose of this book is to understand a precarious present, and warn against a fatal future.

Fall, Spring, and Winter

The deafening shots of gunfire caused some in the crowd to run and others to stop in their tracks. Suddenly, amid the commotion, Neda Agha Soltan fell to the ground. Distraught friends and concerned strangers—among them a doctor—rushed to try and keep the young woman alive in time for an ambulance to arrive.

The date was June 20, 2009. The event was a mass demonstration against the rigged results of the Iranian presidential election, held eight days earlier. Though opposition candidate Hussein Mir Mosavi clearly had come out ahead of incumbent Mahmoud Ahmadinejad, the latter declared victory and hailed his reign as the "will of the people."

Millions of Iranians of all walks of life took to the streets of Tehran and other cities to protest the false claims on the part of the regime they had intended to replace with what they believed would be a more democratic one. Neda, 26, was among them. Ironically, the recently engaged-to-be-married, aspiring musician and singer, who lived in a modest apartment in Tehran with her mother and sister, was not a political activist. In fact, she hadn't even cast a ballot in the election whose results she was contesting. But she was, according to her family, a "rebel from birth." The first girl in her school to shed her chador and get away with it, Neda (whose name in Persion means "voice") had always sought to be free of the shackles of her sex in the repressive society in which she was raised. That the results of the election had been stolen was enough to get her to join her countrymen at the rally.

She invited three friends to go with her. Braving the muggy, late-afternoon summer heat, the four young Iranians set out in Neda's car. Because her air-conditioner was faulty, the group decided to park several blocks away from the area in which the main action was taking place, and walk the rest of the way.

As they approached, they stopped to observe the crowd, some of whom were running to escape clouds of tear gas used by the police to disperse the otherwise peaceful demonstration. Unbeknownst to the onlookers, they, too, were being watched—by sniper Abbas Kargar Javid, standing on a nearby rooftop. Without hesitation, the member of the Basij paramilitary force aimed and fired his weapon at Neda.

Though Javid later claimed he had not intended to kill Neda (or not *specifically* Neda), his presence there—like that of hundreds of other members of the state-run Revolutionary Guards' militia—was no accident. As soon as protests erupted over the June 12 election results, Ahmadinejad was not merely livid; he also knew he had to act. Any and all public expressions of anti-regime sentiment had to be dealt with, fast and furiously.

As a former revolutionary himself, Ahmadinejad was all too aware that, once allowed to rear its ugly head, dissent has a way of mushrooming. The Iranian president could not tolerate anything that might endanger his own power or the 30-year mullah-led stronghold over the people of Iran—people who had been showing clear signs of wanting to extricate themselves from the Muslim tyranny once so antithetical to their culture.

As was the case of previous demonstrations—such as in 1999, with the closing of reformist newspaper *Salam*, and in 2003, when protests against high tuition costs at Iran's universities turned into a public outcry for democratic reforms[1]—the regime responded to this one with violence, sending the Basij out to the streets to terrorize the demonstrators by shooting at them from any and every direction.

"Neda, don't die!" moaned the young woman's music teacher, one of the acquaintances who had accompanied her to the event and witnessed her being shot in the chest. "Stay with us!" others screamed. A doctor on the scene applied pressure to her wound, to keep her from bleeding out.

But to no avail. The protester who unwittingly would become the literal and figurative face of Iran's "Green Revolution" was dead within two minutes. The last words she managed to utter before losing consciousness were, "I'm burning; I'm burning..."

Immediately, mobile phone photos of the beautiful young Iranian lying on her back with her eyes open and streams of blood trickling from her nose and the side of her mouth were posted on the Internet. Real-time graphic footage of her murder went viral. Computer geeks across the United States began to assist the Iranian rebels to circumvent the jamming of their access to the Web—their main weapon against Basij bullets. Major networks in the US and Europe picked up the story and ran with it.

"We are all Neda," became the motto of the protesters. It was printed beneath the famous photo on posters, T-shirts and other paraphernalia. For a few weeks, it looked as though the Iranian regime was actually suffering the kind of blow that had been hoped for by anyone averse to the use of military force against Iran's nuclear facilities—the kind that happens from within.

Ahmadinejad knew a danger sign when he saw one. Himself a member of the "student" revolutionaries who had fought to oust the Shah of Iran in 1978, he was all too aware of the power of mass enthusiasm where toppling a regime was concerned. The last thing in the world he needed at this point was to have a martyr on his hands—and one who represented a mass movement aiming at a counterrevolution, to boot.

His first order of business, then, was to forbid Neda's family from giving her a proper burial. She could occupy one of the many empty graves dug by regime henchmen for dead protesters, he determined. No customary funeral would be tolerated; the family could not post death notices around their home; and no memorial services in her honor would be allowed in mosques. Failure on the part of her family to abide by these rules would result in arrest and severe punishment.

Both the doctor who tried to treat her on the scene and her fiancé were threatened (the latter taken into custody and beaten), and fled the country out of fear for their lives. The doctor, an Iranian residing in Britain (in Tehran on a work-related trip) returned to England. Her fiancé escaped to Canada.

The state-run media began circulating articles refuting the facts of the incident. Making all kinds of claims, ranging from accusing Western spies of having done the shooting, to asserting that Neda wasn't really dead, the government mouthpieces attempted to blacken the reputation of the woman and her family in every way possible.

On June 29, nine days after Neda's killing, a state-run "vote recount" was completed. Conducted by Iran's Guardian Council and electoral board at the behest of Supreme Leader Ayatollah Ali Khamenei (who just happened to have declared Ahmadinejad's victory a "divine assessment"), its conclusion was to be expected: Ahmadinejad was the true winner.[2]

Shouts of "death to the dictator!" and *allahu akbar!* could be heard from balconies throughout the Iranian capital. Placards denouncing

Ahmadinejad and his regime were carried through the streets. Though the chants were mostly in the protestors' native Farsi, the signs were all written in English—a testament to their desperation to be understood across the globe, especially in America. Their message was succinct and clear: "Neda is all of us."

Obamacare?

On the other side of the world, US President Barack Obama made it his administration's business to observe the lead-up to and aftermath of the Iranian elections with impartiality. Obama himself had entered the White House only five months earlier, pledging to overturn his predecessor's policies. Among these was George W. Bush's position on radical Muslim regimes and groups in general and on the Islamic Republic of Iran specifically. Believing that the only way to rid Iran of its nuclear and hegemonic ambitions would be by extending goodwill gestures to its leaders, Obama abandoned the term "axis of evil," which Bush had coined to define state sponsors of terrorism. Iran, of course, was the prime example. Convinced, as well, that the United States had become a pariah nation in the eyes of the rest of the world for being a capitalist, imperialist bully, the new president was on a purported path to altering all that. His motto was "hope and change": hope for the international community that America would change for the better.

The way to accomplish this, in Obama's view, was through dialogue and diplomacy. The logic was simple enough: America would show itself to be in no way superior to other countries and cultures. In return, those other countries and cultures would be willing to exchange their resentment for friendship, and their bombs for olive branches—even the fast-nuclearizing Islamic Republic.

Indeed, in an act of serious "outreach," Obama prepared a videotaped message in honor of the Iranian New Year, during the month of March— three months before the Iranian presidential election. Reiterating much of what he had said in his inaugural address two months earlier, the president appealed to the "people and *leaders* [emphasis added] of the Islamic Republic of Iran" as follows:

"We [the US and Iran] have serious differences that have grown over time. My administration is now committed to diplomacy that addresses the full range of issues before us, and to pursuing constructive ties among the United States, Iran and the international community. This process will not be advanced by threats. We seek, instead, engagement that is honest and grounded in mutual respect."

This "engagement," as both Obama and Secretary of State Hillary Clinton continued to stress throughout the pre-election period in Iran, would take place between Washington and Tehran, regardless of the election's outcome. The people of Iran, they said, have to "choose" their government—and it's no business of America's which government that is or may turn out to be.

On June 12, as Iranians went to the polls, the American president held a press conference in the Rose Garden.

"We are excited to see what appears to be a robust debate taking place in Iran," he said, in response to a reporter's question. "...And whoever ends up winning the election in Iran, the fact that there's been a robust debate hopefully will help advance our ability to engage them in new ways."

For her part, Secretary of State Hillary Clinton—also talking to reporters—said she was encouraged by the size of the Iranian voter turnout.

"It's a very positive sign that the people of Iran want their voices and their votes to be heard and counted," she said.

As it would emerge in the coming days, no "robust debate" or desire on the part of the Iranian public to have "their voices heard and their votes counted" made the slightest bit of difference. The people had spoken, but what they were saying—that they wanted to replace Ahmadinejad with Moussavi—was unacceptable to the clerical thugs running the country.

In an act of bravery under such circumstances, the Iranian people vociferously backed Mosavi when he contested the falsified returns. At great risk to their personal safety and to that of their families, they flooded Facebook and stormed their streets. The government responded with brutality, detaining opposition leaders, curbing the press, jamming Web access and arresting, beating, and shooting demonstrators.

But the Obama administration remained purposely silent. Since its policy was to engage the Iranian regime no matter what, there was no point in antagonizing Ahmadinejad or the ayatollahs by taking a stand that could jeopardize future "dialogue."

As a result, Washington adopted a neutral stance.

On June 13, Clinton said: "We are monitoring the situation as it unfolds in Iran but we—like the rest of the world—are waiting and watching to see what the Iranian people decide. The United States has refrained from commenting on the election in Iran. We obviously hope that the outcome reflects the genuine will and desire of the Iranian people."[3] On the same day, White House spokesman Robert Gibbs stated that the administration was "impressed by the vigorous debate and enthusiasm that this election generated, particularly among young Iranians."

On June 14, Vice President Joe Biden gave an extensive interview to David Gregory on NBC's *Meet the Press*, during which he grudgingly admitted that there might be cause for concern, both about the validity of the Iranian election results and about the regime's response to the resulting public outcry. However, he basically wanted to make clear that it was too early to tell what was really going on in the Islamic Republic.

When asked by Gregory whether he considered Ahmadinejad to be the rightful winner of the election, Biden's tongue-tied answer was: "Well, you know, we don't have all the details. It sure looks like the way they're suppressing speech, the way they're suppressing crowds, the way in which people are being treated that there's some real doubt about that. I don't think we're in a position to say."

Gregory: "You sound like you have doubts."

Biden: "Well, you know, I, I have doubts, but I—we're going to withhold comment until we have a, you know, a thorough review of the whole process and how they react in the aftermath... there are an awful lot of questions about how this election was run. And we'll see. I mean, we're just waiting to see. We don't have, we don't have enough facts to note—to make a firm judgment."

Gregory: "Even without those facts, the question is whether the belligerence we're seeing from Ahmadinejad is a sign that he is emboldened, that this regime is emboldened, or is it in some way weakened? ..."

Biden: "Well, the question is, is it for domestic consumption or is it for foreign consumption? It's obvious he has some problems right now. Let's assume he won the election fair and square, he still has some problems at home. And so it seems as though he—it—you know, it's hard to say where it's directed. It could just as easily be directed at his domestic critics. And they are, they are real..."

Gregory: "But this administration went out of its way—the president sent a message directly to the Iranian people; the president made this speech in, in Cairo[4] reframing the relationship with the Muslim world, and yet this is the response from the Iranian people. Or is it?"

Biden: "Well, well..."

Gregory: "Do you think Iran is a democracy?"

Biden: "No. That's the question, is this the response, is this the accurate response we're getting? Is this the result of the Iranian people's wishes? The hope is that the Iranian people, all their votes have been counted, they've been counted fairly. But look, we just don't know enough..."

Gregory: "Who runs Iran's nuclear program?"

Biden: "Well, look, this is a regime, it's not a single person. The supreme leader is, by all accounts, the supreme leader. And so I doubt whether there's anything that can be done without—of consequence—without the supreme leader's sanctioning."

Gregory: "If these results are borne out, if Ahmadinejad remains in power, this administration has said it's willing to engage with Iran. How do you go about doing that?"

Biden: "Look, talks with Iran are not a reward for good behavior. They're only a consequence if the president makes the judgment it's in the best interest of the United States of America, our national security interests, to talk with the Iranian regime. Our interests are the same before the election as after the election, and that is we want them to cease and desist from seeking a nuclear weapon and having one in its possession, and secondly to stop supporting terror. That's why we've joined with the so-called P5+1[5]. We've laid out to the Iranian regime what it is that we, the P5+1, are prepared to talk about. And, and look, we—if there are talks, we are, you know, it's something that is going to be done with the regime. It's not being done with a single person... Look, the decision has been made to talk. We've laid on the table a proposal to the Iranians saying we are ready to talk. And we've indicated we'll fully participate in that. We're ready to participate, we're ready to talk."

On June 15, a day after Biden's interview, Obama had a sit-down with CNN. With characteristic finesse, he managed to present a position and its opposite simultaneously.

"Obviously all of us have been watching the news from Iran," he said.

"And I want to start off by being very clear that it is up to Iranians to make decisions about who Iran's leaders will be; that we respect Iranian sovereignty, and want to avoid the United States being the issue inside of Iran, which—sometimes—the United States can be a handy political football, or discussions with the United States."

He went on: "Having said all that, I am deeply troubled by the violence that I've been seeing on television... And whenever I see violence perpetrated on people who are peacefully dissenting, and whenever the American people see that, I think they're rightfully troubled. My understanding is that the Iranian government says that they are going to look into irregularities that have taken place. We weren't on the ground, we did not have observers there, we did not have international observers on hand, so I can't state definitively one way or another what happened with respect to the election, but what I can say is that there appears to be a sense on the part of people who are so hopeful and so engaged and so committed to democracy, who now feel betrayed. And I think it's important that, moving forward, whatever investigations take place are done in a way that is not resulting in bloodshed and not resulting in people being stifled in expressing their views."

And then came the real clincher—the reiteration of the president's determination to conduct "dialogue" at all costs.

"Now, with respect to the United States and our interactions with Iran, I have always believed that, as odious as I consider some of President Ahmadinejad's statements, as deep as the differences that exist between the United States and Iran on a range of core issues, that the use of tough, hard-headed diplomacy, with no illusions about Iran and the nature of the differences between our two countries, is critical when it comes to pursuing a core set of our national security interests," he said, explaining, "Specifically, making sure that we are not seeing a nuclear arms race in the Middle East triggered by Iran obtaining a nuclear weapon; making sure that Iran's not exporting terrorist activity. Those are core interests not just to the United States but, I think, to a peaceful world in general."

And how would he achieve such a goal? By continuing "to pursue a *tough direct dialogue* [emphasis added] between our two countries, and we'll see where it takes us. But even as we do so, I think it would be wrong for me to be silent about what we've seen on the television over the last few days, and what I would say to those people who put so much hope and energy and optimism into the political process, I would say to them that the world is watching and inspired by their participation, regardless of what the ultimate outcome of the election was. And they should know that the world is watching, and particularly to the youth of Iran, I want them to know that we in the United States do not want to make any decisions for the Iranians, but we do believe the Iranian people and their voices should be heard and respected."

On June 16, responding to critics—most notable among them Senator John McCain, who had lost the US presidential election to him in November—Obama reasserted his non-interventionist attitude to the events in Iran.

"It is not productive, given the history of US-Iranian relations, to be seen as meddling, the US president meddling in Iranian elections," he said. "What I will repeat, and what I said yesterday [in his CNN interview], is that when I see violence directed at peaceful protesters, when I see peaceful dissent being suppressed, wherever that takes place, it is of concern to me and of concern to the American people."

He did not specify whether this "concern" would translate into action on behalf of the Iranian people, if at all. Nor did he indicate whether it would affect his determination to jump-start negotiations as soon as the dust settled and bodies were buried.

On June 22, Obama again gave a press conference in which he reiterated his position/non-position on the matter.

"Well, look, we didn't have international observers on the ground," he said, to Huffington Post reporter Nico Pitney (whom he had phoned earlier in the day to tell him to ask the question he did[6]). "We can't say definitively what exactly happened at polling places throughout the country. What we know is that a sizeable percentage of the Iranian people themselves... consider this election illegitimate... And so, ultimately, the most important thing for the Iranian government to consider is legitimacy in the eyes of its own people, not in the eyes of the United States. And that's why I've been very clear: ultimately, this is up to the Iranian people to decide who their leadership is going to be and the structure of their government."

The only way he could think of to assist the Iranian people in such a daunting endeavor was as follows: "What we can do is to say unequivocally that there are sets of international norms and principles about violence, about dealing with peaceful dissent, that spans cultures, spans borders. And what we've been seeing over the Internet and what we've been seeing in news reports violates those norms and violates those principles."

He concluded his remarks by indirectly appealing to the sensibilities of the Islamic Republic's leadership. "I think it is not too late for the Iranian government to recognize that there is a peaceful path that will lead to stability and legitimacy and prosperity for the Iranian people," he said. "We hope they take it."

The chance that the mullah-led Ahmadinejad regime would forfeit even one iota of its power, or care about the "stability" and "prosperity" of its people, was nil, as anyone familiar with its radical ideology could have, would have, and should have known. But acknowledging this fact would be as uncomfortable to Obama as the video of Neda Soltan's murder, on which he was forced to comment the following day.

On June 23, during a general White House press briefing (which included his discussing unemployment rates among African-Americans and Latinos), the US president appeared ill at ease when asked whether he had seen the footage of Neda's killing.

Nodding repeatedly, he said, "It's heartbreaking; it's heartbreaking. And I think that anybody who sees it knows that there's something fundamentally unjust about that."

In answer to a follow-up question relating to the source of the gradual letting-up of the protests, he said, "Yes. I have concern about how peaceful demonstrators and...uh...people who want their votes counted may be stifled from expressing those concerns. I think, as I said before, there are certain international norms of freedom of speech, of freedom of expression, and I think it's important for us to make sure that we let the Iranian people know that we are watching what's happening, that they are not alone in this process. Ultimately, though, what's going to be most important is what happens in Iran. And, you know, we've all been struck by the courage of people. And I mentioned this, I think, in a statement that I made a couple of days ago. Some of you who had been covering my campaigns know that this is one of my favorite expressions, was Dr. [Martin Luther] King's expression that 'the arc of the moral universe is long, but it bends towards justice.' We have to believe that ultimately justice will prevail."

Within less than a week, Iran's Supreme Leader officially declared Ahmadinejad the rightful winner of the election. Protests began to fizzle out, as more opposition leaders and supporters were jailed or otherwise silenced. So much for justice having prevailed for Neda and the rest of the "courageous" Iranians to whom the president of the United States had paid lip-service. The "Green Revolution" had not merely wilted; it had been mown down.

Sparks from Tunisia

Six months later, on December 17, 2010, a Tunisian street vendor named Mohamed Bouazizi doused himself with paint thinner and lit a match. The self-inflicted blaze that would end the life of the 26-year-old produce peddler has been considered the catalyst for what came to be called the "Arab Spring."

Many if not most Americans had barely heard of Tunisia before this incident. Those who had would have been hard put to locate it on a map. Even many Tunisians themselves were less than familiar with the town of Sidi Bouzid, where the horror took place. It was here where Bouazizi was born, raised, and lived in a small house with his five siblings, mother and step-father—his uncle, whom she married after his father died when he was a toddler.

Within hours of his self-immolation, however, this impoverished rural community became the focusus of attention at home and abroad, and Bouazizi's plight emerged as the symbol of uprisings that would sweep across the Middle East in the days, weeks, and months to follow.

Bouazizi was lucky to have any income at all in this area with nearly triple the overall 14 percent unemployment rate and university graduates who had no hope of finding work. Bouazizi did not have an academic degree. For the seven years prior to his suicide, he had supported himself and his family by selling fruits and vegetables from a cart. His highest aspiration was to save enough money to purchase—or at least rent—a pick-up truck to expand this endeavor. To call this aim of his a pipe dream would be a gross understatement, and not only because the earnings with which he fed eight people never amounted to more than about $50 per month. In addition, he had regularly been subjected to harassment on the part of local inspectors, the purpose of whose claims that he lacked a proper peddling license was to have their palms greased with weeks' worth of his livelihood.

But this is the norm for citizens living under autocratic regimes, like that of Tunisian President Zine El Abidine Ben Ali: rampant abject poverty for those citizens not part of or in with the autocratic, violent and corrupt top echelons, and no recourse or freedom to improve their lot.

Bouazizi, then, usually succumbed to his fate by keeping as low a profile as possible, then putting up and shutting up when accosted—until the fateful day in question, that is. On that particular Friday morning, the young vendor suffered the kind of slight to his honor that no Muslim-Arab man is taught to tolerate: he was spat at, insulted and slapped... by a *woman*. That this particular lady was a police officer made the sting all the more potent, precisely because there was no way he could fight back. To make matters worse, she was accompanied by a couple of male colleagues who kicked him, both literally and figuratively, while he was down. And all this because he tried to prevent them from taking away the apples and cucumbers he was trying to sell to passers-by for a pittance, as well as the small scale he used to weigh the produce.

With his body bruised, his pride injured and his cart confiscated, Bouazizi decided to take legal action. But when he arrived at the municipality to lodge a complaint, he was refused entry. It was at this point that he went to fetch a canister of fuel, then returned to the premises and set himself on fire.

His grieving mother would tell *Time* magazine's Rania Abouzeid that "Mohammed did what he did for the sake of his dignity."[7]

Whether Bouazizi's slow and excruciating death in the hospital over the next two and a half weeks repaired Bouazizi's wounded dignity is unclear. What is certain is that it enflamed far more than his own flesh.

News of his desperate act swept not only his own small town through word of mouth and via the Internet, but throughout Tunisia.

Citizens across the country began hailing his "martyrdom" as an act of personal bravery and public salvation. As though taking a cue from the 1976 classic film *Network* (in which Americans follow the ranting of a frustrated-to-the-point-of-deranged anchorman, and begin screaming out of their windows, "I'm as mad as hell, and not going to take it any more!"), Tunisians began to take to the streets in protest against Ben Ali and his regime.

Nor was the Tunisian leader deaf to these cries. In an effort to try and ease the genie back into the bottle, Ben Ali himself appeared at Bouazizi's bedside at the Burn and Trauma Center in Ben Arous—with a camera crew, a check for 1,000 dinars (roughly $720) and a promise to Bouazizi's distraught mother to do everything he could to help her son and investigate the incident.[8]

This gesture, which took Ben Ali a full two weeks to extend, was perceived by the public as "too little too late," and no more than a cynical, self-serving photo-op. Bouazizi finally succumbed to his injuries on January 4. Ten days later, as posters of Bouazizi were going up across Tunisia, those of Ben Ali were being torn down. His 23-year reign had come to an abrupt end.

White House Watch

Across the ocean, US President Barack Obama was undoubtedly thrown for a loop. How should he respond to this turn of events, if at all? Whose side should he be on?

On the one hand, his equivocal reaction to the protests in Iran six months earlier had proven problematic. It had garnered him much criticism, even among his own supporters both inside and out of the administration. It had left Ahmadinejad's reign of terror to quell the rebellion.

Yet it had not led to the regime's desire to enter into any "dialogue" with the US regarding the nuclear program.

On the other hand, unlike Ahmadinejad, the Tunisian president was a long-time US ally, one famous for bettering his country's economy and keeping Islamic terrorism at bay. Still, his people were taking to the streets and demanding freedom from oppression—or at least that's what they came to call what they were *actually* demanding, taking their cue from Western terminology spread on the Internet and in international media outlets. What they were initially bemoaning was the hopelessness of their financial plight—with a corrupt leader who was keeping all the wealth to himself, and reserving all the jobs for his cronies and relatives. Bouazizi's act of desperation had given these frustrated citizens something concrete to rally around. Surely the American leader would have to take a stand, one way or another, especially at this point in time.

As luck—or fate—would have it, just as Bouazizi was becoming a household name, Obama staffers were on the verge of completing an analysis of the Middle East.

According to a highly publicized *New Yorker* article by Ryan Lizza[9], by the end of the summer, when the protests in Iran had subsided or gone underground, Obama sent a long memo to senior members of his administration and foreign-policy team about trends in the Arab and Muslim world. The August 19 memo, titled "Political Reform in the Middle East and North Africa," spelled out the president's thoughts on how the US should confront the "growing citizen discontent with the region's regimes."

Fearing that "increased repression could threaten the political and economic stability of some of our allies, leave us with fewer capable, credible partners who can support our regional priorities, and further alienate citizens in the region," Obama stated that America's "regional and international credibility will be undermined if we are seen or perceived to be backing repressive regimes and ignoring the rights and aspirations of citizens."

According to Lizza, who obtained a copy of the memo and spoke about it to a number of White House officials, "Obama instructed his staff to come up with 'tailored,' 'country-by-country' strategies on political reform. He told his advisers to challenge the traditional idea that stability in the Middle East always served US interests. Obama wanted to weigh the risks of both 'continued support for increasingly unpopular and repressive regimes' and a 'strong push by the United States for reform.'"

A group was then assembled to "test assumptions" and "challenge conventional wisdom" in relation to each country in the Middle East and North Africa, and prepare an in-depth report on their findings.

The three people charged with heading this task were: Samantha Power, head of the National Security Council's Office of Multilateral Affairs and Human Rights; Gayle Smith, responsible for global development, stabilization and humanitarian assistance issues at the NSC; and Dennis Ross, special adviser to Clinton for the Persian Gulf and Southwest Asia. As Lizzy describes it, "Soon, they and officials from other agencies were sitting in the White House, debating the costs and benefits of supporting autocrats. A White House official involved said the group studied 'the taboos, all the questions you're not supposed to ask.' For example, they tested the assumption that the President could not publicly criticize President Hosni Mubarak because it would jeopardize Egypt's cooperation on issues related to Israel or its assistance in tracking terrorists. Not true, they concluded: the Egyptians pursued peace with Israel and crushed terrorists because it was in their interest to do so, not because the US asked them to.

"They tested the idea that countries with impoverished populations needed to develop economically before they were prepared for open political systems—a common argument that democracy promoters often run up against. Again, they concluded that the conventional wisdom was wrong. 'All roads led to political reform,' the White House official said."

It was with these conclusions in mind—ones that have been proven wrong since the eruption of the Arab Spring and henceforth—that Obama greeted Bouazizi's death and Ben Ali's downfall.

Nevertheless, in the true spirit of the "leadership from behind" in which this president prides himself, it wouldn't be until the day of Ben Ali's departure for refuge in Saudi Arabia that Obama would release a public statement expressing his full-fledged support for the ouster.

"...The United States stands with the entire international community in bearing witness to this brave and determined struggle for the universal rights that we must all uphold," he declared. "...Each nation gives life to the principle of democracy in its own way, grounded in the traditions of its own people, and those countries that respect the universal rights of their people are stronger and more successful than those that do not. I have no doubt that Tunisia's future will be brighter if it is guided by the voices of the Tunisian people."[10]

Obama's public abandonment of Ben Ali, and his pronouncement that "each nation gives life to the principle of democracy *in its own way, grounded in the traditions of its own people*," [emphasis added] couldn't have been clearer signals to the rest of the Muslim world's leaders and citizens. Washington was going to view and treat popular rebellions across the Middle East as freedom-fighting, democracy-seeking, "we-want-a-better-life" revolutions. This, no matter which groups would be behind the uprisings—and *no matter what their definition of democracy*.

It should have been of little surprise, then, when Algeria suddenly got into the act. Egypt was soon to follow, as was Libya, Yemen, Bahrain and then Syria. Nor was it unexpected that Obama's response, "country by country," would turn out to have been disastrous. This is because it is not *conventional* wisdom that Obama was abandoning, but rather wisdom altogether.

Instead of commissioning a review of the Middle East—whose real purpose was to contradict any and all of George W. Bush's ideas and policies—Obama would have done far better to have his staff give him a history lesson on a very different predecessor: Jimmy Carter.

Indeed, it is the story of the fall of Iran to the Ayatollah Khomeini in 1979 that should be guiding US foreign policy in face of what would be better described as the "Arab Fall," with winter fast approaching.

It is the story of how a US president with a dim view of American power and exceptionalism abandoned a staunch ally in favor of a sworn enemy about whom little was known and even less studied.

It is the story of how a short-sighted leader of the Free World, in an attempt to ingratiate himself with—rather than defeat—the forces that would see him and it destroyed, enabled the rise and spread of a pernicious form of radicalism that threatens the globe to this day. And while it was Jimmy Carter who opened the door to this radicalism in Iran three decades ago, it is Barack Obama whose policies are laying out the welcome mat for it to flourish in the rest of the Middle East today. While it was Carter who sat by and allowed dozens of his embassy staff in Tehran to languish in captivity for more than a year, it is Obama who is sitting by and allowing those former captors to develop nuclear weapons with which to take the region and the world hostage for generations to come.

PART I
THE FALL OF IRAN

CHAPTER ONE

November 1979

On November 1, an estimated two million Iranians converged on and around the campus of Tehran University to demonstrate against the "Great Satan."

Feverish chants in Farsi calling for death to America and its president, Jimmy Carter, amid rapturous screams of *"alluhu akbar,"* permeated the chilly autumn air.

A few miles away, the US Embassy stood virtually empty, save a contingent of Marines on high alert. Its non-essential staff had been given instructions by Chargé D'Affaires Bruce Laingen to remain off the premises for the duration of the rally, lest it get out of hand.

He had reason to worry that it might.

Hysterical, often violent, anti-US protests were not unusual in Iran in those days—certainly not during the tumultuous year prior to the event in question, as the Islamic Revolution began to take hold. And this one was of particular significance.

Ten days earlier, President Carter had allowed the self-exiled, cancer-ridden Shah, Mohammed Reza Pahlavi, to enter the United States for medical treatment.

The otherwise rival Iranian revolutionary groups that had united under the extremist Shi'ite cleric Ayatollah Ruhollah Khomeini to overthrow the pro-Western Shah and replace his monarchy with an Islamic theocracy took this opportunity, as they had many others before it, to vent their rage. Viewing their former leader as a weak and corrupt puppet of the American government, these groups wanted revenge for the nearly four decades of what the radical Islamists among them viewed as a godless regime and the communists a brutal one. Now they craved the Shah's blood—and his money—and made no bones about it.

They were demanding that Pahlavi be returned to Iran for prosecution, and undoubtedly subsequent execution. Anything short of that would not only be unacceptable; it would serve as additional proof of pernicious American intervention in their private affairs of state.

Unconvinced that the Shah was seriously ill (he had kept his lymphoma a secret, even from his wife, well before he fled), these radicals believed that the US was plotting to return him to his Peacock Throne, with his vast personal assets and military arsenal intact.

Ironically, nothing could have been farther from the truth. By this point, Carter, whose backing of the Shah, even from the outset of his presidency, was equivocal at best, considered the ailing emperor-in-exile to be an outright liability.

"Fuck the Shah," he had responded when implored for the umpteenth time by former secretary of state Henry Kissinger and others not to abandon a faithful ally whose throne was toppled and whose days were numbered. "I'm not going to welcome him when he has other places where he'll be safe."

Pahlavi, then, had no recourse but to accept asylum elsewhere. He wandered from Egypt to Morocco, from the Bahamas to Mexico, and then to Panama.[11]

When Pahlavi first arrived in Egypt, on January 16, 1979, billionaire philanthropist and former ambassador to Britain Walter Annenberg offered him a temporary haven at his luxurious estate near Palm Beach. But the Shah turned down the invitation.

That "suits me just fine," Carter wrote in his dairy. If there was one thing the president did not want it was to have to shoulder any consequences that might ensue from appearing to side with the ousted emperor. "All I need is to have the Shah here playing tennis while Americans in Tehran are being kidnapped or killed," he said.

But as the months dragged on, and the Shah's physical condition deteriorated, so did pressure mount from inside and out of the administration to let him in to the United States.

"I never had any ambiguity about the Shah," Kissinger told me in an interview in his New York office. "Once the crisis developed, one should have known that Khomeini would undermine the progress and orientation of Iran, where I had always thought it was in our interest to preserve a friendly government. Indeed, I thought this was the best opportunity, eventually, for it to develop into a democratic society."

On April 8—three months into the Shah's exile, Kissinger phoned the president and urged him to reconsider his position. Carter refused.

The former secretary of state let him have it a few hours later, in front of a packed audience. In a speech he delivered that evening at the Harvard Business School, Kissinger rebuked the president for treating the Shah like "a Flying Dutchman who cannot find a port of call."

Not long afterwards, Vice President Walter Mondale and National Security Advisor Zbigniew Brzezinski joined Kissinger and others— such as Chase Bank chairman David Rockefeller, whose financial dealings with the Shah had led to a long-standing friendship—in their pleas on behalf of the homeless monarch.

Even Hamilton ("Ham") Jordan, Carter's closest aide and confidant, began to beg him to change his mind. Kissinger, Jordan argued, would not let up. And in the event that the Shah died without receiving proper treatment in an American hospital, the former secretary of state would hold him responsible—and do so publicly. Jordan tried to impress upon his boss how little the administration could afford such negative PR.

"To hell with Kissinger," Carter reportedly replied. "I am president of this country."

Nevertheless, Carter finally caved in a few months later. In October, he permitted the Shah to fly to New York for surgery. But he wanted to make it crystal clear to Khomeini and the provisional government in Tehran that his change of heart was due solely to compassion for a dying man.

Any support beyond that, he felt, would not only endanger the lives of Americans stationed in Iran; it would make it well-nigh impossible for him to persuade members of the revolutionary regime of his genuine good will towards them. In keeping with his overall foreign policy, what Carter most sought at this juncture was dialogue.

Indeed, on the very day of the demonstration in question, he sent Brzezinski to meet with Iranian interim Prime Minister Mehdi Bazargan, foreign minister Ibrahim Yazdi and defense minister Mostafa Chamran in Algeria. This was his way of sending a signal that he was interested in finding common ground with the *current* government in Tehran, fuck the Shah.

But Khomeini wasn't buying anything Uncle Sam had to sell. In the first place, he hadn't been informed of the Algeria meeting until after it was over. In the second, as far as he was concerned, no move on the part of the Great Satan was anything other than an attempt at subversion.

Ditto for the protesters swarming the streets of Tehran. When they got wind of the "secret" summit in Algeria, their rampant suspicions were vindicated. Wasn't this hard evidence of an American conspiracy? Wasn't it a perfect example of history's repeating itself?

Fresh in their minds was the 1953 CIA-assisted overthrow of Mohammed Mossadeq, the Iranian prime minister who would come to personify opposition to the Shah in particular and the West in general. During the coup d'état, sparked by two years of conflict between Britain and Mossadeq over the latter's nationalization of Iranian oil, the Shah absconded to Italy. Upon completion of the coup, dubbed "Operation Ajax," the then 27-year-old Pahlavi flew home to reoccupy his palace. Upon his return, he announced gratefully to CIA Middle East division head Kermit Roosevelt, Jr.: "I owe my throne to God, my people, my army—and to you!"

As if that declaration alone were not enough to give credence to the notion that the American espionage agency was responsible for the next two and a half decades of Pahlavi's rule, it was the CIA who had helped establish and train the Shah's security force, SAVAK.

Though a full 26 years had passed since Operation Ajax, its lore was alive and well in the collective psyche of the demonstrating masses, many of whom had suffered at the hands of SAVAK agents. The "den of spies," as the revolutionaries referred to the American embassy, was a natural target at which to aim their venom. This is why Laingen—a newcomer to his post as acting ambassador, but a veteran foreign-service officer—had taken precautions to have the compound cleared out during the demonstration.

The fact that, by the day's end, the only signs visible at the embassy were epithets spray-painted on its outer walls, alongside a large poster of Khomeini, appeared to be due to acting foreign minister Yazdi's having made good on a promise. He had assured his American counterparts that as long as the Shah refrained from making political statements while in the United States, America's diplomats would be safeguarded.

The embassy staff was relieved. Now they could all go home and enjoy a leisurely weekend. For his part, Laingen was eager to get on with what he had been sent to Iran to accomplish: showing the new government that Washington was friend, not foe—in spite of its previous ties to the now irrelevant Shah.

That was Thursday.

On Friday, Khomeini—for whom the Shah was anything *but* irrelevant—gave a hate-filled speech in which he accused the US of plotting against Iran by "taking in our enemy."

On Saturday, he released a statement calling on "all grade-school, university, and theological students to increase their attacks against America and Israel, to force the US to return the criminal Shah" to Iran.

Unbeknownst to the White House, the State Department, the Pentagon, the CIA, the embassy in Tehran—and even to Khomeini himself—Sunday would mark the beginning of the end of Laingen's optimism... and Carter's presidency.

Light Years of Separation

The time difference between Washington, DC and Tehran is 8.5 hours, a few less than it takes to fly from one capital city to the other. But for all Jimmy Carter seemed to know during his first three years in the White House, Iran may as well have been on Mars. And for all he came to understand during his fourth and final one, it was simply yet another among a long list of countries with legitimate grievances against the super-power whose past mistakes he, as its leader, was determined to rectify.

This is not to say that Carter—a peanut farmer from Georgia who became governor of his state and rose out of nowhere to become America's 39th president—was unaware of Iran's strategic significance. On the contrary, theoretically as much a Cold Warrior as his predecessors, Carter considered any state allied with the US to be crucial in the fight to fend off Soviet aggression. Iran under the Peacock Throne of Pahlavi had been just such an ally for decades. Carter not only knew this, but paid lip service to it on more than one occasion.[12]

Still, as the Islamic Revolution that would oust the Shah in favor of Khomeini began to foment, Carter and his administration were looking the other way. Then, when they finally did realize what was happening, they went so far as to imagine that it could turn out to be a blessing in disguise.

This "blessing" he initially imagined took the form of an interim government, headed by Shapour Bakhtiar. Bakhtiar had been put in place by the Shah prior to his departure for Egypt. He seemed like a good choice for prime minister, since he had been part of the anti-Shah resistance, but also a reformist, and thus might be acceptable to all sides. And though it was Bakhtiar who allowed Khomeini to return to Iran, ordered the SAVAK disbanded, and freed all political prisoners, the ayatollah considered him a traitor for accepting an appointment from the Shah and deemed his government illegitimate and illegal. Unable to garner support from Khomeini or the Iranian masses, Bakhtiar would last only 36 days in his post.[13]

Carter took this to mean that Khomeini really was the people's choice—and that having a venerable religious leader keeping a military or other government's possible human rights abuses in check during this time of upheaval might just have a salutary effect on Iran. Perhaps it would even be beneficial to stability in the region.

To be fair to Carter, a self-described devout Christian—who even continued to teach Sunday school throughout his presidency—the

35

gradually modernizing country that blossomed into the medieval Islamic Republic before his very blind eyes was, indeed, of a completely different species from his own.

Nor was the potent draw that radical Islam would have in the Muslim world as palpable a phenomenon as it soon would become.

In addition, reports that Carter was receiving from his inner circle in Washington and from American personnel on the ground in Iran were often as conflicting as they were inaccurate. This was due to many factors, among them a severe shortage of Farsi-speaking foreign-service personnel and an equal dearth of CIA operatives.

Furthermore, the president had his plate full of other concerns at home and abroad during the period that the Shah was losing his grip. These included: creating the departments of energy and education; bailing out the Chrysler corporation; trying to reform health care; pressuring Israel during its peace negotiations with Egypt; negotiating the second Strategic Arms Limitation Talks with the Soviet Union; making a deal with China; helping the Sandanistas in Nicaragua to overthrow Somoza; relinquishing control of the Panama Canal; and last but not least, trying to ensure his winning reelection in the Democratic primaries against rival Teddy Kennedy after the latter threw his hat in the ring.

It is thus that when he awoke on the morning of November 4—two days before those very primaries—to learn that the American embassy in Tehran had been overtaken by an angry mob of students, the president sighed in dismay. Had his decision to allow the Shah into the US been the right one? He had done all he could to keep the ailing monarch away for the past nine months. Indeed, were it not for incessant pressure from Kissinger, Rockefeller, and others, he would have left well enough alone. The Shah was finished, after all. It was Khomeini with whom he now cared to engage in diplomacy.

As Carter was briefed throughout the day on the details of the siege in progress, he hoped the Iranian powers-that-be would intervene to put a stop to it. There were two reasons for him to harbor such hope.

First, a similar incident had taken place six months previously, on February 14, just after Khomeini's return to Iran following fifteen years of forced exile by the Shah. During that event, which left the embassy bullet-riddled and two Marines wounded, the Iranian authorities acted swiftly, ending the takeover in a matter of hours.[14] Second, the November 1st rally had taken place as scheduled with little mishap, while Brzezinski was making progress in Algeria with Bazargan, Yazdi, and Chamran, each of whom had spent much time in the West.[15]

Yazdi, who, during his years as a Texas-based medical researcher, had acted as the exiled ayatollah's unofficial spokesman in the US, had declared Khomeini a peaceful religious leader seeking freedom and democracy for his people.

When Khomeini returned to Iran, Yazdi—who had managed to persuade much of the American media, academia and political establishment that the ayatollah was a champion of human rights—was appointed foreign minister in the provisional government.

Clearly, then, Carter had good reason to trust that his bound and blindfolded embassy staff would soon be unshackled, unharmed. He didn't want even to contemplate what steps he would take if they were not.

"Without the protection provided by the host government," he wrote in his diary that evening, "it's almost impossible to do anything if one's people are taken."

Unfortunately for the hostages, the "host government" Carter was referring to responded to the siege by resigning. So much for whatever progress had been made in Algeria three days earlier, or for guarantees of protection for Americans in Iran.

The writing of this scenario had not only been on the proverbial wall—or on the literal one of the graffiti-marked embassy. In fact, it had filled Khomeini's published works and public statements for all to see and hear. The trouble was that they were not yet translated into any languages other than Farsi and Arabic. In addition, prominent American "Iran experts" and others came out in defense of their author.

Among these was Professor Richard Cottam, noted in *All Fall Down*, a personal, behind-the-scenes account of the American view of the Iranian revolution by Gary Sick, National Security Council staffer and Carter's chief aide on Iran. Cottam, a political science professor at the University of Pittsburgh, was not merely a scholar of Iranian politics and culture; he had also worked for the US government as a specialist in Iranian internal affairs—his first stint there coinciding with Operation Ajax, which he vehemently opposed, and his second three years later.

Sick tells of having been contacted by Cottam in September 1978, suggesting that he meet with Yazdi, Khomeini's representative in the United States. According to Sick, "Cottam argued that Khomeini's positions—apart from his absolute opposition to the Shah—were relatively moderate and deserved a hearing."

Other voices in this chorus abounded, among them those of George Ball and Henry Precht.

Ball, appointed by Carter in November 1978 to head a special White House task force on Iran, recommended that the US stop backing the Shah, and switch its support to Khomeini.

Precht, who headed the Iran desk at the State Department, persisted in his assessment that Khomeini was merely an esteemed religious figurehead, and that the Shah's exit would serve to strengthen the moderates.

On November 9, 1978, US Ambassador to Iran William Sullivan sent a cable offering a similar interpretation. In a memo titled "Thinking the Unthinkable," Sullivan expressed confidence that the Shah's downfall was inevitable, and that a more moderate and democratic regime would replace his monarchy. He based this judgment on a number of premises. One of these was that both the "pro-Western" military and the mullahs were anti-Soviet. Another was that the religious establishment had no institutions in place to govern. As a result, he argued, there would be a mutually beneficial alliance between the two, which would compel Khomeini—who could return to Iran as a "Ghandi-like" figure—to appoint a political leadership acceptable to the military. This, according to Sullivan, would prevent what might have been a tendency towards extremism. As it happened, Carter considered Sullivan to be "insubordinate," and never fully trusted the ambassador's take on the climate in Iran. He had far more faith in General Dutch Huyser, whom he would dispatch to Iran a few months after Sullivan wrote his famous memo.

Huyser was deputy commander-in-chief of the US European Command. Once in Iran, where it was his task to keep informed of the goings-on in the Iranian military, he became what Carter considered to be a more reliable source of information than the ambassador. Though Huyser did not believe that Khomeini would bring democracy to Iran, he did suggest that a takeover by the ayatollah would lead to a communist regime.

Right around that same time, in January 1979, Ramsey Clark, former US attorney-general under President Lyndon Johnson, embarked upon a private, eight-day fact-finding mission to Iran. At the end of the trip, he stopped over in France to meet the ayatollah-in-exile. He was accompanied by Richard Falk, professor of international law at Princeton University, and Don Luce, a prominent member of "Clergy and Laity Concerned," an organization established in 1965 by the National Council of Churches, "...not simply [to] end the war in Vietnam, but [to] struggle against American imperialism and exploitation in just about every corner of the world... to join those who are angry and who hate the corporate power which the United States presently represents, and to attempt, in our struggle, to liberate not only black, brown and yellow men in every corner of the world, but more importantly, to help liberate our own nation from its reactionary and exploitative policies."

Upon his return to the US, at a press conference held on January 22 at the offices of the National Council of Churches in New York City, Clark referred to Khomeini as a "brave man" for having been the first to openly oppose the Shah. He also pooh-poohed Bakhtiar as unpopular, asserting that "99 percent of the Iranian people" supported Khomeini. He then conveyed a message to Carter and the American people on behalf of the "religious leader," asking that the internal affairs of Iran not be tampered with. "Let the nation determine its own fate," Clark quoted Khomeini.[16]

On February 8, a week after Khomeini's return to Iran from exile, Carter's close associate and ambassador to the UN, Andrew Young, went a bit beyond the call of duty in relation to the ayatollah. At a meeting with the New York Forum, a group of reporters at the City Graduate Center, Young called Islam "a vibrant cultural force in today's world;" attributed the Shah's downfall not to an excess of modernization but of repression; and hinted that American support for the Bakhtiar government was misplaced. "Khomeini will be somewhat of a saint when we get over the panic," he said. "In two years, our relations with Iran will be on a pretty even keel."[17]

James Bill, an Iran specialist at the University of Texas who acted as an adviser to Carter, also put in his two cents. In an interview with *Newsweek* on February 12, he called Khomeini a man of "impeccable integrity and honesty."

Prof. Richard Falk, who had traveled to Iran and then to France with Ramsey Clark, published an op-ed in *The New York Times* on February 16, called "Trusting Khomeini." In the piece, Falk waxed poetic about the Muslim cleric, disabusing readers of the notion that the oft-regarded "mystery man" was someone to be feared either by Iranians or by the

West. "The depiction of him as fanatical, reactionary, and the bearer of crude prejudices seems certainly and happily false."

Falk went on to laud the progressive and benevolent nature of Shi'ite Islam. "What is distinctive, perhaps, about this religious orientation," he wrote, "is its concern with resisting oppression and promoting social justice."

He concluded that, "Despite the turbulence, many non-religious Iranians talk of this period as 'Islam's finest hour.' Having created a new model of popular revolution based, for the most part, on non-violent tactics, Iran may provide us with a desperately needed model of humane governance for a third world country."

In hindsight, then, one could forgive Carter for taking a more benign view of Khomeini than the aging cleric warranted. One could understand the president's determining that if this venerable religious figure was going to be pulling the strings in Iran, the US might as well as accept it and get on with forging crucial ties with him.

Or could one?

Renowned Orientalist, professor emeritus of Near Eastern studies at Princeton Bernard Lewis doesn't think so.

"In 1978, there was this figure being discussed, Khomeini, whom I knew nothing about," he recounted to me during a recent interview at his home near the camp. "So I did what one normally does in my profession: I went to the university library and looked him up. I discovered that he was the author of a book called *Islamic Government* [a collection of speeches he made in Najaf, Iraq, in 1970]. And I thought, 'Well, this is interesting. It could give me some idea of what the man is about.'"

Lewis took the volume home and read it in one sitting. What it revealed was a philosophy of Islamic statehood, using the harshest possible rhetoric to denounce non-Muslims, and calling for the spread of Sharia law across the world.

Deciding that something had to be done to expose the ayatollah and his intentions, Lewis contacted *New York Times* op-ed editor Charlotte Curtis and offered to write a piece on the book.

"No thanks," she answered. "I don't think our readers would be interested in the work of some Persian writer."

Whether this response was due to the editor's ignorance of the significance of the ayatollah waiting in the wings to take over Iran from the Shah or a lack of desire on the part of the *Times* to acknowledge that however authoritarian a ruler the Shah may be, he was the epitome of benevolence compared to what would follow is not clear. Nor did Curtis's attitude surprise Lewis, whose view of the press was already quite dim.

It did cause him, however, to remember an exchange he had had in Pahlavi's office not long before the revolution.

"Why do they keep attacking me?" the Shah burst out, as soon as Lewis entered the room.

"Whom do you mean, Your Majesty?" Lewis asked.

"*The New York Times, The Washington Post, The Times of London,* and *Le Monde*—the four weird sisters dancing around the doom of the West," Pahlavi said. "Don't they understand that I am the best friend you have in this part of the world?"

"Your Majesty," Lewis replied, "you must understand that the editorial policies of these papers, like the foreign policies of Western powers, are based on Marxist principles."

"What do you mean?" Pahlavi shot back incredulously. Whatever else he might have faulted the West for, Communism wasn't on the list.

"I'm not referring to Karl," Lewis quipped, "but rather Groucho."

When the Shah looked puzzled, Lewis asked him whether he was familiar with Groucho Marx.

"Yes, of course I am," he responded, almost insulted by the very suggestion that he might not be up on Hollywood.

Lewis explained: "Remember when Groucho Marx said: 'I wouldn't want to become a member of any club that would have me?'"

"Yes..." Pahlavi hesitated, not yet getting the connection.

"Well, our media's posture—like our foreign policy—is to shun any government that wants our friendship, and to placate and pursue our enemies."

Khomeini, Lewis concluded early on, was just such an enemy. And he made it his business to delve more deeply into the writings of this elderly ayatollah, fast emerging as a force to be reckoned with both in Iran and on the world stage.

Political scientist Richard Perle (who would come to serve as assistant secretary of defense in the Reagan administration) remembers receiving a phone call from Lewis later that year, after an anchorman on the evening news called Khomeini a "shadowy figure." At the time, Perle was on the staff of Senator Henry "Scoop" Jackson.

"Bernard said, 'If I see another reference to this 'mysterious' figure, the Ayatollah Khomeini, I'm going to scream. There is nothing mysterious about him. He's written four books. Let me read you something from the most recent one.' Lewis has what came to be known as the *Little Green Book* in front of him. He's on the phone in Princeton; I'm in Scoop's office in DC. And he starts reading these blood-curdling passages about Sharia law and radical Shi'ite Islam, which most people in America hadn't ever heard of before. So I said, 'This is really important stuff. You've got to write something on it.' I suggested he write an op-ed for *The New York Times*, in which he quotes extensively from Khomeini's book. He said he had already tried that and failed. I told him to go ahead and write it anyway; I would help him get it published. So he did. I then sent the piece to my old friend, Judy [Judith] Miller, at the *Times*. She thought it was terrific. We both assumed the *Times* would want it. But she called me a couple of days later to say that the *Times* wouldn't publish it, because Khomeini's people in Paris were claiming the book is a forgery—and that Khomeini never said the things attributed to him. When I called Bernard with this update, he was already way ahead of me. 'Copies of the book are disappearing off library shelves all over the US and Europe,' he informed me. Clearly, Khomeini's advisers understood that this book would not go down well in the West."

Perle then asked Lewis to send him a copy of the book. If he could get it authenticated, maybe the *Times* would reconsider publishing the piece. When the book arrived in the mail, Perle called Jack Maury at the CIA, the liaison officer between his organization and the Senate.

"Jack," he said, "I've got this book here by the Ayatollah Khomeini. Could you have your guys at the Iran Desk attach a little note saying it's an authentic publication?"

"Sure," Maury answered. "That should be easy."

Or so he thought.

A few days later, Maury reported back to Perle. "There's a problem," he said. "None of our guys is familiar with the book, and they're not prepared to state that it's genuine."

Still, though Lewis's piece didn't make it into the *Times*, Judith Miller did end up publishing a news feature based on its contents, as did other "whistle-blowers."

One of these, US foreign policy expert and Iran specialist at the Foundation for the Defense of Democracies Michael Ledeen relays the same experience.

"Three of us in Washington—Judy Miller, [Washington Post columnist] Steve Rosenfeld, and I—got translations of Khomeini's sermons and writings. Each of us, separately, wrote the same piece in different newspapers. What we said, essentially, was, 'You don't like the Shah? Fine. But this guy Khomeini is going to be a lot worse. Worse for us, worse for the Iranians, worse for the region, worse, worse, worse. Look at what he's advocating!' The CIA's response was: 'We are unaware of any writings by Khomeini, and we'd rather think that this stuff is really disinformation.'"

That the Iran Desk at the CIA, "at a moment when, arguably, it was their single most important priority to understand what was going on in Iran, not only had not read this book themselves, but didn't know enough about it even to know they could read and judge its authenticity for themselves" was so mind-boggling to Perle that it caused him to grimace during our interview in Washington. "So much for our intelligence agency," he said.

Indeed, this is the very organization that in August 1978—a mere six months before Khomeini's triumphant return as head of the revolution—reported that Iran was "not in a revolutionary or even pre-revolutionary situation."

It is no wonder that there was such a complete miscalculation on the part of America's espionage agency. In an article in the December 2009 issue of *Commentary*—"The 35-Year War on the CIA"—Arthur Herman gives a chilling account of how the organization's wings were steadily clipped, to the point at which it barely functioned. When Carter took office in 1976, he joined in the New Left witch-hunt. He, too, considered the CIA dangerous, both inside the US and out—responsible, among other things, for America's reputation abroad as an "evil empire." He was determined to finish the task, already underway, of neutering the agency. To this end, he issued an executive order severely curbing its activities, limiting its powers and making it answer to eight different Congressional committees. He also supported the Foreign Intelligence Surveillance Act, passed by Congress in 1978, requiring that a panel of judges pre-approve all covert surveillance.

As far as Carter was concerned, Admiral Stansfeld Turner couldn't have been a better choice to head the organization-in-transition. The two seamen had met at the US Naval Academy in the 1940s. (Subsequently, Carter served for six years on ships and submarines in the Atlantic and Pacific fleets; Turner went on to become the commanding officer of a guided missile cruiser, commander in chief of NATO Southern Flank and then president of the Naval War College.)

Turner's views made him suitable for the job. He held that modern technology had rendered the need for intelligence-gathering agents in the field obsolete. He also believed that "openness" was the key to achieving peaceful relations among nations across the globe. The CIA, he felt, should "shift its attention from 'out-of-date' concerns like the Cold War, to new, more humanitarian activities like predicting crop failures in the Third World."[18]

Turner's contribution to Carter's castration of America's covert activities was to fire a whopping 800 operatives.

Israeli Warnings Aside

Israeli ambassador to Iran Uri Lubrani during the period in question recalls trying to warn his American counterparts about the fall of the Shah and what would ensue.

"A year before [the revolution], I felt that something was going to happen," he said in a recent interview at his home. "I didn't know what, but I knew it would be substantial, and no one believed me. Later, the Americans interrogated me to find out where I had gotten my information, and I couldn't explain to them that it was an accumulation of information, experience, and feelings. Intelligence services don't like this, because they want proof of everything. And nobody at the time who sensed imminent danger had actual proof."

Though it seemed that "actual proof" arrived as soon as the Air

France jet delivering Khomeini back home landed in Tehran on February 1, it would take the American administration many months to realize or acknowledge that the events surrounding his return were not temporary.

True, both the US and Israel evacuated hundreds of their nationals as a safety measure. But both countries left a number of officials in their embassies. The logic behind this policy was that, however skeletal their staffs may have to be for a while, at least they constituted a presence on the ground.

For Israel, that presence would be extremely short-lived. On February 10, thousands of revolutionaries, chanting "Death to Israel!" and "Long live Arafat!" stormed the Israeli Embassy. As the frenzied mob climbed over the walls, looted the property and burned its flag, its remaining staff members escaped out of a back gate, and ran for their lives.

That afternoon, Arafat, who was making an "official" visit to the new regime in Tehran, took over the now empty building, declaring it Palestinian Liberation Organization headquarters. As a PLO flag replaced the torched Israeli one, Arafat announced from the embassy's balcony: "Under the ayatollah's leadership, we will free Palestine!"

Meanwhile, the embassy personnel—before boarding a plane leaving Iran a week later—took refuge wherever they could find it in the city.

General Itzik Segev, the last Israeli military attaché to serve in Iran, also looks back on America's blindness during that period with a mixture of disgust and amazement.

"When our embassy was attacked, the US ambassador and military attaché came to my house," he recounted. "'You are in danger,' they warned. 'Come stay with us.' I said, "If I do that, they'll attack you, too—don't you get it? But they scoffed at the very suggestion. 'Attack *us*?' they said in disbelief. They didn't consider this to be even a remote possibility."

Segev never took them up on their offer. But the US Embassy was attacked four days later anyway.

As a representative to the peace talks between Israel and Egypt that continued after the signing of the Camp David Accords (on September 17, 1978), Segev met Carter in the United States some months after fleeing Iran.

Referring to him as a "card-carrying idiot"—one who "was more suited to be a pope in Rome than a president in Washington"—Segev bemoaned the lack of the former American leader's understanding of the way things work in the Middle East in general, and in Iran in particular.

He described a large dinner party where he was seated with Prof. Itamar Rabinovich (who would become Israel's ambassador to the US more than a decade later), Jimmy and Rosalyn Carter, Gerald Ford and his wife, Ambassador Andrew Young and his wife and Saudi Prince Bandar, who successfully lobbied the US Congress for the sale of F-15s to Saudi Arabia, and who would become the Saudi Ambassador to the US in 1983.

"We had barely sat down and Carter said to me, 'General Segev, I would like you to tell everyone at the table how I managed to eradicate the evil SAVAK.' I said to him: 'Mr. President, do you think this is the right time and place? People are about to eat.' He said, 'Yes, yes. I would really like you to.' I had a minute to think about it, and decided to tell him exactly what I think—to tell the truth—even if it meant never being invited back. So I did. 'Look,' I said. 'The Shah's SAVAK was very bad. Its people tortured and killed. But what you have replaced it with is a thousand times worse. Its people enjoy death. They shoot you in the legs and then five hours later they shoot you in the gut. Only after fully enjoying watching you suffer and bleed do they finish you off by shooting you in the head.' Itamar Rabinovich kicked me under the table. Everyone stopped eating."

Taking America Hostage

November 4 was selected as the day on which a fledgling group calling itself the "Muslim Students Following the Imam's Line" would execute a carefully laid plan to overtake the US Embassy. The date had both symbolic and logistical significance. It marked the 15-year anniversary of Khomeini's forced exile by the Shah (it was on Nov. 4, 1964 that the ayatollah left Iran, first for Turkey, then to Iraq, and finally to France); and a year since a student demonstration quelled by the Shah left many protesters dead. Subsequently, November 4 was declared National Students Day. The mass demonstration scheduled to commemorate both events would be a perfect cover for the Muslim Students Following the Imam's Line. They could make their move on the embassy unnoticed among the throngs of activists from all of Tehran's institutions of higher learning that would be filling the streets of Tehran. Early that morning, the key organizers gathered in a room at the Islamist Abu Kabir University to outline their plan to the hundred other students who would be among those carrying out the siege. Maps of the embassy buildings were laid out and pored over; specific tasks were assigned to each participant. The idea was to break in to the 27-acre compound and take the embassy staff hostage for three days. During this non-violent "set-in" (as the students mistakenly pronounced "sit-in"—the term they adopted as reminiscent of American camp demonstrations in the 1960s), they would demand the return of the Shah for the purpose of his being meted out a fitting measure of justice.

The purpose of the siege, many weeks in the making, was multi-faceted. It would serve as a symbolic assertion of Islamic victory over American power. It would send a message to the West that the Iranian people would not rest until the Shah was brought to justice. It would demonstrate utter loyalty to Komeini. And it would signal to the members of Bazargan's interim government—which the group considered treasonous for its behind-the-scenes dealings with the Great Satan— that any interference on their part in the operation would pit them against the "imam" and his devoted followers.

Among these followers was 23-year-old Mahmoud Ahmadinejad, a student of civil engineering at the Iran University of Science and Technology. As a member of the pro-Khomeini umbrella organization "Strengthen the Unity," Ahmadinejad had been approached at the plan's inception. He had proposed taking over the "Marxist anti-God" Soviet Embassy instead, but was outvoted.[19] This was not only because the others considered America to be the greater Satan of the two superpowers. It was also clearly due to an unspoken understanding that the Russians would treat such an event as an act of war, and would respond by killing all the attackers on the spot. The United States, on the other hand—as had been proven during its embassy takeover in February—was far more likely to rely on the Iranian government to deal with and put an end to the aggression.

Though the students did not reveal their plan to Imam Khomeini, they did run it by another respected religious leader, Mousavi Khoeniha. Khoeniha opted for a "don't ask, don't tell" policy in regard to the ayatollah. He was certain that Khomeini would not disapprove of the action once it was underway, but would be put in a bad position vis-à-vis the Bazargan government if he were requested to give the green light in advance.

Another potential hurdle the students anticipated was the reaction to the siege on the part of the Iranian security forces. This they overcame by informing the police and Revolutionary Guards of their intentions, and by receiving reassurance that they would be left alone to carry out their mission. To distinguish themselves from the masses of other demonstrators—and make themselves visible to one another— this particular group of young activists would wear laminated photos of Khomeini around their necks. The women, clad from head to toe in traditional Islamic garb, would hide tools and other paraphernalia under their chadors: bolt and chain cutters to break through the main gate of the embassy; rope for scaling the walls and binding the hostages; strips of cloth for blindfolds; and knives and guns to make it possible. That the hostage-takers would outnumber the embassy staff was not enough of a guarantee of success. It would all depend on the response of the "spies" in the evil den.

The stage now set and the actors acquainted with their parts, the only real question remaining was whether blood would be spilled by the end of Act One. If it were their own, so be it. Martyrdom in the name of Allah would not be too a high price for their endeavor; it would be the ultimate honor.

As anticipated, hordes of protesters began to disperse across the city. Though clothes were dampened from the morning drizzle, spirits were not. The thrill of a successful revolution was in the air. On days like this, disparity disappeared. Shared hatred of the monarchy and the West created the exuberance of unity. "Death to the Great Satan!" they shouted, as they burned American flags and effigies of the president. "Death to Jimmy Carter—give us the Shah!"

Getting ready for their usual Sunday-morning meeting, the embassy staff could hear the rise and fall of the ranting outside the windows of their offices on the compound—which had been fortified with bars, following the February 14 takeover.

It seemed, at first, to be nothing more than a repeat performance of a few days earlier. Today, as then, it would turn out to be much ado about nothing. As embassy security chief Al Golacinski pointed out, the Students Day demonstration was "not aimed at us."[20]

There was no reason, then, for Chargé d'Affaires Laingen not to keep his appointment at the Iranian foreign ministry that morning. On the

contrary, it was contact such as this that he was sent to Tehran to culti-
vate. He and his Farsi-speaking assistant, Victor Tomseth, were accompanied by Golacinski's assistant, Mike Howland, who was advised to take
them on a circuitous route, so as to avoid the mobs already amassing
on the main streets.

At 10 a.m., an estimated 100-200 Muslim Students Following the
Line of the Imam broke into the embassy. Some cut the chains securing
the main gate; others bolted it shut behind them. Watching on in awe
were thousands of other demonstrators, who then began to follow suit
by scaling the walls and other gates of the "den of spies." Within hours,
there were some 3,000 students inside. True to their word, the Iranian
security forces whose job it was to protect the outer perimeters of the
compound did nothing.

Nor were any US Marines anywhere near the entrance. They witnessed the break-in on closed-circuit TV. Immediately, they grabbed
their weapons, took up positions and waited to see what would happen—and what, if anything, they could or should do about it.

The students, who had familiarized themselves with every inch of the
compound—both from maps and from observation up close while waiting
in line for bogus visa requests—spread out in search of soon-to-be captives. They knew that most would be located at the chancery, the large edi-
fice just inside the main gate. They also knew that it was the best secured
building of the compound, as it housed the most important documents.

The personnel who had come outside to see what was going on
were grabbed, tied up and blindfolded, in spite of their protestations
of having their diplomatic rights violated. While their hostage-takers
escorted them to a different building, others worked to break into the
basement of the chancery, cutting through locks and prying open the
bars on the windows.

The Marines waited at the top of the stairs, cocking their weapons.

As a group of students began climbing towards them, they fought back with warnings and tear gas. But to no avail. The hostage-takers had been prepared to take bullets for their cause.

This would prove to be unnecessary, however. At this moment, Gola-cinski, who had gone outside to reason with the students, was grabbed, bound and blindfolded. With a gun to his head, he was commanded to give the order to the Marines to hold their fire.

Meanwhile, another group of embassy staffers was holed up in a secure room of the chancery, where most of the documents were stored and now being destroyed to prevent them from falling into the hands of the Iranians. In this room, there were telephones whose lines had not been cut. Some of the staffers were giving ongoing updates to Laingen at the Foreign Ministry, while Ann Swift, the head of the embassy's political section, was reporting to Washington. Outside the door of the room, the hostage-takers were demanding to be let in, and threatening to kill those Americans already abducted.

It began to dawn on the embassy staff that they were in actual physical danger—and that no help was on the way. But by this time, the Marines had been told to get rid of their weapons, and Laingen had instructed Swift to open the door and let the captors in.

"Surrender with your head held high," Howland, who had taken the phone from Laingen at the Foreign Ministry, told the military liaison officer, now surrounded by frenzied Iranians.

In an interview in Laingen's home in Bethesda, Maryland, I asked the former acting ambassador and hostage why he ordered the Marines at the embassy not to shoot and the rest to surrender.

"According to the traditions of American diplomacy," he said, "force is only to be used in extreme cases."

Did this not qualify as an "extreme case"?

"This has to be considered in the context of where it was, and how practical it was," he explained. "I thought using force would be impossible to do without a lot of loss of life. I didn't want my staff to get riddled with bullets. Jimmy Carter didn't want it."

As for whether action on the part of the Marines might have scared off the hostage-takers—all university students—Laingen thought not. "Well, we'd had the experience of the embassy takeover six months earlier," he pointed out. "And they didn't appear to be scared *then*."

It is thus that by nightfall, the students-turned-hostage-takers had fulfilled their dream. As Carter would comment two days later, they had managed to grip the United States "by the balls."

Washington Wakes Up, Snoozing

The next morning, Carter was not overly concerned that about 60 people in his embassy in Tehran had spent the night on cold floors, without being able to see—or allowed to speak to—one another. "The students are still holding our people with the public approval of the idiot Khomeini," he wrote in his diary, before covering other events he seemed to consider of no less importance.

While he was signing the Gas Rationing Act and ordering an investigation into increasing Klu Klux Klan activity, his national security adviser, Zbigniew Brzezinski, was convening the first meeting of the Special Coordination Committee (SCC), established to handle what would come to be known as "the hostage crisis."

According to Gary Sick, who attended the meeting, "It was agreed that utmost caution should be exercised in any public US statements to avoid making the situation worse. The SCC recognized the need to communicate directly with Khomeini and his religious circle, and it was recommended that a special emissary be sent to Iran."

It was decided that former attorney general Ramsey Clark and staff director for the Senate Select Committee on Intelligence William Miller would be a perfect duo for the task. Clark had already been impressed by the ayatollah in France, and had returned conveying a message from him to the president and the American people.

Miller, too, had been a Khomeini apologist. Who better to make a pilgrimage to the chief mullah proud of his flock for holding American hostages than they?

That night, they were summoned to the State Department for a briefing prior to their trip to Qom, where Khomeini was based. They were to deliver a letter from the president to the ayatollah, and try to get the hostages released.

The letter—written on White House stationery—was addressed to "His Excellency Ayatollah Khomeini."

It read as follows:

"Dear Ayatollah Khomeini,

"Based on the willingness of the Revolutionary Council to receive them, I am asking two distinguished Americans, Mr. Ramsey Clark and Mr. William G. Miller, to carry this letter to you and to discuss with you and your designees the situation in Tehran and the full range of current issues between the US and Iran.

"In the name of the American people, I ask that you release unharmed all Americans presently detained in Iran and those held with them and allow them to leave your country safely and without delay. I ask you to recognize the compelling humanitarian reasons, firmly based in international law, for doing so.

"I have asked both men to meet with you and to hear from you your perspective on events in Iran and the problems which have arisen between our two countries. The people of the United States desire to have relations with Iran based upon equality, mutual respect, and friendship.

"They will report to me immediately upon their return."

The typewritten epistle was hand-signed "Sincerely, Jimmy Carter."

"His Excellency" never got the opportunity to read or respond to the president's plea. This is because he refused to allow Ramsey and Miller into Iran. As suitable as the pair may have been in terms of their hostility to the Shah and dim view of America's international relations, in Khomeini's eyes they were merely representatives of the Great Satan. As such, they didn't deserve the time of day, let alone an audience with the holy Imam.

That fact would only become known to Carter two days later. In the meantime, he was anxiously following the Congressional elections held on November 6. Of these he wrote, "Democrats did very well all over the country, electing governors in Kentucky, Mississippi. The press interpreted the southeastern state votes as a victory for me against some strong Republican challenges."

His pleasure at this outcome was marred by the resignation that day of the Bazargan government, however, which he had prayed would intervene on behalf of the hostages. And since a military or rescue operation was a last-resort option as far as he was concerned, the leader of the United States of America—one of the world's two superpowers—felt he had no choice but to look elsewhere for assistance.

"We...asked the Algerians, Syrians, Turks, Paks, Libyans, PLO, and others to intercede on behalf of the release of our hostages," he wrote in diary that evening. "It's almost impossible to deal with a crazy man, except that he does have religious beliefs and the world of Islam will be damaged if a fanatic like him should commit murder in the name of religion against sixty innocent people. I believe that's our ultimate hope for a successful resolution of this problem."

Seeing an opportunity to ingratiate himself with Carter, PLO chief Yasser Arafat rushed to prove his clout with the Iranian revolutionary regime, with which he had close ties, among them military ones. The arch Palestinian terror master, who despised the Shah for supporting Israel, publicly offered his mediation services to the US government. Not as publicly, but eagerly nevertheless, the White House gave Arafat the heads up.

Arafat had reason to want to help Carter. This was the president who made Palestinian rights a focal point of the Camp David Accords between Israel and Egypt, signed that March. This was the president who had been sick about his UN ambassador having been forced to resign over meeting clandestinely with the head of the PLO. If he could make himself a major player in the hostage crisis, Arafat would have better leverage for achieving his true goal—which he was vague about in English, but clear about in Arabic—to replace the Jewish state with a Palestinian one.

Carter, who considered Arafat's organization the "key to any comprehensive [Middle East] peace agreement," and found it "absolutely ridiculous that we pledged under Kissinger and Nixon that we would not negotiate with the PLO," thought it couldn't hurt to have the group's help getting the hostages released. But, as chummy as Arafat may have been (or thought he was) with Khomeini and his henchmen, he was as powerless as the American president when it came to striking a deal that would benefit the Great Satan in any way.

Still, Carter did not give up hope of solving the hostage crisis through diplomatic means. His main objective was to get the hostages out alive and well. Aware that this might not be possible, he had to consider what punitive measures to adopt in the event that they were killed, either one at a time or all together. According to Sick, Carter "said he had thought seriously about the issue and he did not incline to any action that would get the United States bogged down militarily in Iran, where extrication of US forces would be difficult and any pullback would be viewed as a defeat."[21]

Apparently, the president did not think that diplomacy as a means of retaliation for his embassy being overtaken would be "viewed as a defeat."

Indeed, as Sick writes: "The result was an onslaught of messages, pleas, statements, personal emissaries, condemnations, and resolutions of all kinds from governments, institutions and individuals around the world, descending in torrents on Iranian officials and representatives wherever they might be."

This "diplomatic offensive" did not have the desired effect on Khomeini, who summoned his authority and took his cues from Allah, not the United Nations. Nor did it prevent pro-Khomeini Iranian nationals studying in the US from staging demonstrations in support of the hostage-taking in Tehran. These were held in several American cities, among them Washington, DC.

This made Carter angry. His response was to tell his staff to forbid any future such displays where he could see them. When a rally was held the very next day in front of the White House, he vented his rage by insisting even more sternly that his orders be obeyed. He simply couldn't afford to have the public, desperately worried about the fate of fellow Americans in Tehran, see him unable even to stop guests in their country from thumbing their noses in his face. Freedom of speech aside, there had to be a legal way to prohibit or penalize this kind of behavior at such a sensitive time.

His attorney general, Benjamin Civiletti, recalled the difficulty involved: "There were somewhere near 60,000 Iranian students in the United States, mostly on educational visas. The White House made inquiries regarding actions that could be taken against [them]. The students had legal rights and could not simply be locked up or denied those rights just because they were Iranians. They had rights to public assembly, for example... It was a very tough time, because generally

I had to advise the White House that no stringent steps or measures could be taken against these students. What we did do was investigate them individually to make sure they were here legally. We interviewed about 40,000 students, and those in violation of the law had their visas revoked and faced deportation."[22]

Not all of those students supported either the revolutionary regime or the hostage-taking, however. And there was no guarantee that those whose visas were revoked were among the pro-Khomeini activists. Nor did this have the slightest effect on the ayatollah or on the students laying siege to the embassy—other than to believe it was good for their image in the media. It also led to a kind of street vigilantism among some Americans, who went after protesters with baseball bats, and hurled epithets at any passerby who looked like he might be Iranian.

No More Nice Guy?

As the days went by, Carter was growing more and more perturbed. But he was relieved that he wasn't being blamed for lack of progress in getting the captives released.

"I met with family members of the American hostages in Iran," he wrote in his diary on November 9, "who issued a beautiful statement supporting what I'm doing and calling for the American people to be calm."

That same day, according to Gary Sick, "reports began circulating in international financial circles that Iran intended to pull its deposits out of US banks."

The Treasury immediately stepped up efforts to use legal channels to freeze all such assets.

On November 11, an AP photo, which has since become famous,

showed one of the hostages, CIA communicator Jerry Miele, being paraded around the embassy courtyard—his entire face covered with a blindfold, and his wrists tied together—held at his elbows by two student hostage-takers. One of these not only appears to be current Iranian President Mahmoud Ahmadinejad, but has been deemed as such by his captors.

On November 12, Carter announced that the US would cease importing oil from Iran.

On the morning of November 14, Carter gave the final order for the freeze of assets. He also had a lawsuit prepared to file with the International Court of Justice on the state-sponsored hostage-taking in Iran.

On November 17, Iran announced that it would be releasing all the blacks and women hostages not deemed spies.[23]

This had nothing to do with Carter's actions. It was a move by Khomeini to garner sympathy in the American media and public. Well aware of the political climate that put the unknown Georgia governor in the White House in the first place (i.e. disgust with the Vietnam War, the Watergate scandal, and a rise of left-wing radicalism across college campuses,) the ayatollah emphasized his dedication to the "downtrodden and oppressed" minorities. Sending the black and women hostages back to America, he thought, would surely turn them into emissaries for his cause.[24]

As for the remaining hostages, on November 18, Khomeini made what Carter referred to as a "confusing statement" about putting them on trial, implying that if the Shah were not returned immediately to Iran for prosecution, the outcome would be dire. Carter was worried. What would he do if these people were tried, convicted and possibly put to death?

This called for serious action. The form it took was a series of private meetings which Secretary of State Cyrus Vance held with UN Secretary

General Kurt Waldheim. These resulted in a four-point proposal presented to Iranian Acting Foreign Minister Abolhassan Bani-Sadr via intermediaries in New York. The proposal, which took Iran's grievances into account while requesting the release of the hostages, was what Vance hoped would be the basis for negotiations between the United States and the Islamic Republic. And it was, to some extent, throughout the entire 444 days of the hostage crisis. The only problem was that it was never quite clear with whom the Americans were negotiating at a given moment, or whether those Iranians had the authority to make deals.

Indeed, no sooner had Bani-Sadr begun to draft counter-proposals and discuss coming to the Security Council to finalize an agreement for the release of the hostages by the end of the month, he was replaced as foreign minister by Sadegh Ghotbzadeh—whom Carter referred to in his diary as "Iran's Jody Powell."

The Great Mosque Attack Fallout

On November 20, as thousands of Muslims were on their annual hajj (pilgrimage) to Mecca in Saudi Arabia, a group of radical insurgents attacked the Great Mosque. These radicals were claiming that their leader, Abdullah Hamid Mohammed Al-Qahtani, was the true Mahdi—the redeemer of Islam, whose return Muslims pray and wait for—and that he must be obeyed.

The radicals entered the mosque and killed its imam just as he was about to begin morning prayers. They then took hundreds of worshipers hostage, and killed members of security forces who tried to stop them. The siege, which lasted two weeks, ended after Pakistani commandos were allowed by Saudi officials to storm the mosque. By the time the incident was over, hundreds of people were dead and wounded. The 67 perpetrators were subsequently beheaded publicly in four Saudi cities.

On the first day of the siege, Khomeini told radio listeners throughout Iran that "It is not beyond guessing that this is the work of criminal American imperialism and international Zionism."

The next day, on November 21, a mob of students in Pakistan, carrying posters of Khomeini, attacked the US embassy in Islamabad, and burned it to the ground. (An identical incident would take place a week later in Tripoli, Libya.)

Carter understood that Khomeini's statement was inflaming the region. Saudi Crown Prince Fahd told American officials that killing insurgents is a good way to handle sieges. But Carter had other ideas.

On November 23, he told Vance "to notify Khomeini through sure channels that any trials of our hostages would result in severe restrictions on Iranian commerce, that no negotiations through the UN would be conducted, and that any harm to our hostages would result in direct retaliatory action …[and] to notify the four leaders in Japan, France, Germany, and Great Britain that this message was delivered to Khomeini."

On November 27, the black and women hostages who had been released told of their captivity: that they "had been threatened with loaded guns, kept bound, not let speak a single word, not let go outside, bathe, or change clothes."[25]

On November 28, the day that "Iran's Jody Powell" replaced Bani-Sadr as foreign minister, Carter gave a press conference, the purpose of which, he said, was "to show firmness and resolve, encourage Americans to have patience, let the Islamic world know we have respect and reverence for their religious beliefs, and isolate Khomeini as one who believed in kidnapping, extortion, blackmail, and the abuse of innocent people."

By the last day of November, the situation was as follows: There were 53 Americans being held at gunpoint at the embassy; six, who had escaped, were being given asylum by Canadian Embassy staff; and another three—including Laingen—who had gone to the Foreign Ministry on the first day of the siege. Though at first they did not realize that they themselves were also hostages, it became apparent when the Bazargan government resigned, and they were moved to and locked in a room where they would remain as captives, like the rest of their peers, for the next year and three months.

CHAPTER TWO

December 1979

The first days of December in Washington were devoted to relocating the Shah. Finally deemed well enough to travel after receiving treatment at New York Hospital-Cornell Medical Center, the question now was where he would go. The Mexican government, which had claimed that it would allow Pahlavi to return to his place of refuge in Cuernavaca after undergoing surgery in the United States, reneged on its offer as the date approached.

This sudden development not only threw Carter for a loop; it underscored the ever-widening gap between two conflicting positions within the administration. On one side was the view that the best way to handle international relations in general and the hostage crisis in particular was through quiet diplomacy and gentle persuasion. On the other was the more hard-line stance, according to which America had to flex its muscles, rather than allow threats to its security or honor to dictate its policies. Secretary of State Cyrus Vance represented the former. National Security Adviser Zbigniew Brzezinski espoused the latter. Vance's stance tended to reflect Carter's, particularly during the first months of the crisis. On the issue of what to do with the Shah at this juncture, however, it was "Zbig," not "Cy," who got his way.

Though Carter, like his secretary of state, blamed Pahlavi's presence for the escalation in tensions between the US and Iran, he nevertheless decided to keep him on American soil until other arrangements could be made. This was not in deference to Brzezinski, about whom Carter wrote in the Dec. 1-2 entry in his diary: "Zbig has been too much a part of the David Rockefeller community and has always wanted the Shah to stay in this country."

It was, rather, the result of other concerns.

"The situation is that I want him [the Shah] to go to Egypt, but don't want to hurt Sadat," Carter noted. "Sadat wants him to stay in the United States but doesn't want to hurt me. It's a decision for me to make. I called Fritz [Vice President Walter Mondale] re two basic options: Egypt or one of our military bases. Fritz preferred Egypt. [Secretary of Defense] Harold Brown reported either Fort Sam Houston or Lackland Air Force Base—both near San Antonio [Texas]—would be best if we have to keep him here. I told Cy not to talk to me any more about it, but to move the Shah to Lackland, and it was done."[26]

This temporary solution would turn out to pay off for the troubled president. His reward would come in the form of criticism lodged at him by his key political contender within the Democratic Party. On December 3, Ted Kennedy made a statement condemning both the Shah and Carter for housing him. Such sentiments didn't go over big in the public, by then focused on their fellow citizens in captivity overseas.

Americans didn't know much about foreign countries in those days, certainly not about Iran—other than its fame for producing beautiful carpets. What they did know was that an act of unprecedented aggression against their embassy had taken place. This was not merely an attack on a building; it was an attack on the United States as a whole. They felt it was a time for national unity, and for rallying around the president. Kennedy's behavior at this juncture, then, seemed to do almost as much harm to him as a candidate as the Chappaquiddick scandal he had barely weathered nearly ten years before.[27]

Carter couldn't have been more pleased when the media gave attention to Kennedy's words, as well as to Harris poll results showing the president a few points ahead.

The fact that the US Embassy in Tripoli was attacked and burned on December 2 by a frenzied mob of Lybians accusing the Great Satan of having been behind the seizure of the Grand Mosque in Mecca did not make a dent in his view that the Shah was the problem. This act of aggression, on the heels of the burning of the Embassy in Islamabad just under two weeks earlier, caused Carter to withdraw all American personnel in Lybia and shut down the embassy.[28]

Somehow, that particular event did not make it into Carter's diary. Nor did the fact that the Ayatollah Khomeini was just appointed "Supreme Leader" according to the newly forged Iranian constitution get a mention. What *did* was his December 4 announcement "as a candidate for reelection in a heartwarming small ceremony"—as his assertion that stronger economic measures would be needed to pressure Iran over the hostages, while letting *"the world of Islam know we are not at odds with them* [emphasis added]."

Reality TV

It's hard to remember the days before cable and the Internet, but in 1979, the only sources of news were papers, radio, and a handful of television networks, none of which provided round-the-clock coverage of unfolding events the way they do now.

When the hostage crisis began, the president of ABC news, Roone Arledge, saw an opportunity to increase his network's ratings in relation to rivals NBC and CBS. ABC was lagging behind the others, particularly, but not exclusively, in terms of its news coverage, and Arledge made a decision that would alter the face of TV news. He decided to run a nightly program devoted specifically to the hostage crisis, to air at 11:30 pm, right after the local news. In the same time slot on NBC was the hugely popular *Tonight Show* with Johnny Carson, with its host's famous comedic monologues and array of celebrity guests.

The program, first broadcast on the fifth day of the embassy siege, was called "The Iran Crisis—America Held Hostage." It was initially hosted by "World News Tonight" anchor Frank Reynolds. Shortly after its inception, it was given to the network news's State Department correspondent, Ted Koppel, who introduced the format of announcing the number of days the hostages were in captivity at the end of every segment.[29]

Arledge's decision would pay off, big-time. It was a bold move that would become the precursor to the kind of in-depth reportage—replete with color, opinion and debate surrounding a story—we have come to take for granted. To this day it is used as an example of the way in which news shapes public awareness about an issue and vice versa.

The interest in the hostage crisis caused Americans to tune in to Koppel every night, and Koppel kept that interest alive and kicking.

He was unwittingly assisted in this endeavor by Laingen's wife, Penelope, who tied a yellow ribbon around a tree in the yard of the family home in Maryland to symbolize her struggle to get her husband back safely. She had taken her cue from a hit song—made popular by Tony Orlando and Dawn in 1973—about a man returning home from prison.

"Tie a Yellow Ribbon Round the Ole Oak Tree," then, became the theme of the American people's solidarity with the hostages.[30]

Nor was "Penne" Laingen the only face of the hostages' families. As the identities of the hostages came to be released gradually, reporters from all media outlets began to follow their loved ones. Daily interviews with relatives across the country were a crucial part of the ongoing tragic drama of which Americans couldn't get enough. Suddenly, a place in the world to which most of them had never paid the slightest attention was a key focus of their concern.

Unlike their Iranian counterparts, for whom even ancient history loomed large in their psyche, Americans knew little or nothing about events like the oter of Mossadegh. Nor did they grasp the greater, more fundamental reason behind being called the Great Satan: the very luxury of not having to know too much borne of the genuine freedom they had always enjoyed.

As a result, reactions on the part of the American public—though uniform in terms of worry about and compassion for the hostages—were mixed and often contradictory when it came to reaching conclusions about American foreign policy in general and the Carter administration's behavior in particular. Man-in-the-street interviews regularly included statements from "regular Joes" expressing indignation at America's weak and appeasing posture, on the one hand, while simultaneously opposing military operations that might harm the hostages, on the other.

It was a peculiar response, considering that a mere three years earlier, on July 4, 1976, these same "average Americans"—like the rest of the world—had watched in awe as Israeli commandos carried out the "Entebbe Raid,"[31] rescuing 103 mainly Jewish and Israeli hostages held in Uganda by Palestinian terrorists.

Indeed, "Operation Jonathan" contributed to making that a particularly memorable Independence Day for Americans, who were celebrating the bicentennial of the United States with a mixture of pride and disillusionment. Their country had been defeated in Vietnam; they had lost faith in the presidency, after the Watergate scandal had forced Richard Nixon to resign a year earlier; and they were four months away from the election that would usher Jimmy Carter into the White House, replacing Gerald Ford. Witnessing the Israel Defense Forces storm a far-away country in the middle of the night, and return most of the hostages home safely to Israel and other countries was a morale boost for demo-cratic countries at the start of serious decline in their belief in heroism.

Delta Force Prepares

When Colonel Charlie Beckwith learned of the Embassy takeover in Tehran, he assumed two things. The first was that if the president and his men were going to authorize some kind of military and/or rescue mission in Iran, they would employ the US Army's elite counterter-rorism unit Delta Force—which he had founded and commanded—to carry it out. The second was that they would never really consider such an option.

"Negotiations and compromise are the tools this administration will use," he thought. It "doesn't have enough grit to do anything."[32]

Though this turned out to be an incorrect assessment, as Delta Force was eventually deployed to execute a hostage-rescue operation in April 1980, everything that Carter had done up until that point—including waiting so long—made the mission all but impossible. But this is for later.

When Beckwith was informed that a training camp was to be set up to prepare for a rescue operation in Iran, he was both encouraged and extremely worried. Not only were the hostages located deep in the heart of a hostile country several thousand miles away, but intelligence was almost nil. This was due to the severe curtailing of CIA operatives in the field—cuts, as pointed out earlier, made by director Stansfeld Turner— and a lack of budget for security personnel at foreign embassies.

Indeed, the embassy takeover on the previous Valentine's Day showed how unprepared American security services were both to anticipate and to handle such events.

Beckwith was more of a doer than a thinker. His military career had included many difficult covert operations, each of which required careful and arduous planning. His assumption that the president was not likely to act in this case was similar to that of the Iranian revolutionaries. Their courage, like Beckwith's skepticism, was derived from their having witnessed Carter's inaction six months earlier.

But a lack of intelligence-gathering and presidential will were not the only factors contributing to Beckwith's belief that an operation to rescue the hostages would require nearly super-human feats of prowess.

Wade Ishimoto, Beckwith's chief intelligence officer during that period, explained why this was so. In an interview with "Ish" in Washington, he said that, according to what was called at the time the "critical path methodology program evaluation and review technique"—used as a flow chart for assessing risks—"There were way too many potential failure points."

"We were very limited in our options. Our biggest problem was the lack of close in-launch bases from where we could execute a one-night mission. It couldn't be compared to the Entebbe raid. Though the Israelis had to travel significant distances, they were going up against a very unsophisticated military—Idi Amin's Ugandan forces. This is not to minimize how they planned and executed the mission. But we had a whole different set of problems to contend with. We couldn't get into Afghanistan, which had been invaded by the Soviet Union, because it was landlocked. So we would have to cross, say, Pakistani airspace. We couldn't come in from India, and we couldn't fly over Iran. But within a week or so, our embassy in Islamabad was burned to the ground by militant Islamists. Our relationship with Pakistan in those days was as tenuous as it is today. So Pakistan was eliminated as a potential launch base. Possibly we could have used Jordan, but it had no really developed military bases at that time. We would still have to overfly Iraqi air space, and Iraq was not our friend in those days. Then there was Turkey, where, ironically, a secular government had managed to take hold again. We had bases in Incirlik, for example. But the thinking in the State Department was that if we launched from Turkey, it would cause that secular government to fall."

Of this Beckwith wrote in his memoirs, "In the long haul, [the inability to use Turkish soil] "proved very unfortunate."

Still, from the moment Beckwith was told to prepare for a possible mission, he and his men went into high gear, analyzing each "failure point," proposing possible solutions and selecting and training participants.

William (Jerry) Boykin was one of those participants; he would later become the commander of Delta Force. In an interview with him in Charleston, Virginia, where he resides and teaches, he told me why it was Carter and his administration that were responsible for the eventual failure of the mission.

"We trained with intensity and passion and great hope, but not with expectations," Boykin said. "As the months went on, we reached the point at which we didn't believe Carter would launch the operation— and time was of the essence, due to the change of seasons. We needed many hours of darkness to be able to pull off the mission, and as spring approached, the days grew longer."

Boykin also pointed to Carter's ideology. "He had said upfront, at the very beginning, 'We will do nothing to jeopardize the lives of those hostages,' when what he should have said was, 'All options are on the table.'"

Washington Seeks European Support

On December 4, a full month into the hostage crisis, Carter convened the National Security Council. During the meeting, Carter discussed imposing economic sanctions to exert pressure on Iran to release the hostages. The problem with this measure, he said, was that it would not work without European cooperation.

Because Secretary Vance was going to Brussels the following week to attend a special NATO gathering of foreign and defense ministers to discuss Soviet nuclear proliferation,[33] it was decided that he should use the opportunity to try and garner support for such sanctions among America's allies abroad.

The United States had submitted a petition against Iran before the International Court of Justice on November 29. Carter wanted to have as much European support in place as possible before the Court's delivery of a verdict. The US president believed the Court would rule in America's favor, since the Khomeini-sanctioned hostage-taking was so clearly a violation of international law. But he wasn't so sure about European leaders' willingness to get involved in something that wasn't their problem. One way to achieve this, he thought, would be for Vance to indicate to his counterparts at the NATO meeting that if comprehensive sanctions against Iran could not be agreed upon, the US would be forced to impose a unilateral blockade and consider a military option.

The plan seemed to have worked. By December 15—the day the International Court ruled unanimously in America's favor against Iran—Vance was able to report that the European allies and Japan agreed to help the US obtain a Security Council green light for sanctions. They also agreed to take economic steps independent of the Security Council, in the event that the Soviets vetoed a resolution.

As was expected, Iran rejected the International Court's findings. The US then went into high gear to procure a Security Council resolution. Vance's optimistic tidings aside, American Ambassador to the UN Donald McHenry was having trouble getting the needed support among UN member states.

On December 22, the US submitted a draft resolution calling upon all member states to impose a sweeping embargo on Iran. The Soviet Union, as feared, vetoed the resolution. As far as the US was concerned, this spelled an end to any hope for UN assistance in securing the release of the hostages.

The two Security Council resolutions that did pass, one on December 4 and the other on December 31—calling on the Government of Iran "to release immediately the personnel of the embassy of the United States of America being held in Tehran and to provide them protection and to allow them to leave the country"—had as little effect on Iran as the International Court ruling. "There's nothing America can do," remained the Khomeini-backed slogan of the hostage-takers.

The First Noel

As Thanksgiving had come and gone with no progress in reaching Khomeini to reason with him, the White House feared that the embassy staff was going to be spending Christmas in captivity, as well. While siding with Vance's view that restraint was the best policy, the president made an attempt—feeble in the eyes of the ayatollah—to flex his muscles. This he did by ordering the transfer of six Sea Stallion helicopters to the *S*

Kitty Hawk, which was stationed in the Indian Ocean, and by keeping US AWACS[34] planes in Europe and North Africa, ready to be sent to Egypt in the event that they would be needed in any kind of action against Iran. This did not stop Khomeini from continuing to threaten that if the Shah were not returned home to face charges, the hostages would be put on trial for espionage.

Carter wanted to believe this was a bluff. He took solace in reassurances from Iran's ambassador to the US that "personal trials for the hostages were not a real option," and expressed hope that "this is an accurate report from Khomeini."[35]

In the meantime, he decided to adopt Vance's suggestion that the National Christmas Tree have only its peak star lit, with the others remaining in darkness, as a symbol gesture "until the hostages are released."

This was Carter-the-citizen—waiting like the rest of his countrymen for something to happen, and relying on the media to fill him in on developments. Carter-the-candidate-for-reelection, however, was pleased at this moment.

"An AP and Gallup poll are both surprisingly good for me," he wrote on December 8. "Gallup jumped from 30 percent approval to 61 percent in one month."

Two days later, he added, "The evening news reported that the ayatollah had come out against me for president, which will give another boost to our campaign."[36]

On December 13, Carter's young daughter lit the National Christmas Tree. It was "an emotional experience when Amy threw the switch and the lights did not come on the big tree, except the star of hope at the top," he wrote. "It was on national television, and I got more comments about this than almost anything I've ever done."[37]

With the approach of the holiday, people across the United States began sending Christmas cards to the hostages. School children were encouraged to prepare home-made "Dear Hostage" greetings, all of which included prayers for the recipients' safe and speedy return.

The hostage-takers decided to exploit the "infidel" celebration for their own purposes. Pressured by the international community to allow independent observers to see how the captives were faring, they succumbed. It was, after all, a perfect opportunity to spread their propaganda via the media. To this end, they decided to invite members of the American clergy—in addition to the Catholic cardinal of Algiers—to visit the hostages and attend a Christmas party at the besieged embassy. Three theologically and politically liberal clerics were carefully selected for this purpose by the student captors: the Rev. William Howard, Jr., Monsignor Thomas Gumbleton and the Rev. William Sloane Coffin, Jr.

Howard was the president of the left-wing National Council of Churches. Gumbleton, the Auxiliary Roman Catholic Bishop of the Archdiocese of Detroit, was famous for his anti-war civil disobedience.

Coffin, of New York's Riverside Church, was known by then as an icon of anti-war activism and sympathy to Communism. As a former intelligence agent who resigned from his post at the CIA over the Mossadeq ouster, he couldn't have been a better tool for the Iranian students. They considered him someone who had "seen the light" about America's evils.

Indeed, Coffin had already made public statements sympathetic to them. "We scream about the hostages, but few Americans heard the screams of tortured Iranians,"[38] was one such declaration.

Then, on the eve of his trip to Tehran to conduct services for the hostages, he delivered a sermon attacking the Carter administration's attempt to impose economic sanctions on Iran. Doing so is "highly reminiscent of Lyndon Johnson's bombing of North Vietnam," he said,[39] causing some members of the congregation to storm out of the church in protest.

It made perfect sense for the hostage-takers to want Coffin to lead the Christmas service for the American "spies."

In preparation for the event, several hostages were forced to sign declarations of solidarity with their captors, to be read aloud on camera during the "festivities." Those who refused would not be allowed to partake of the holiday goodies—food the likes of which they hadn't tasted in weeks—spread out for the benefit of the visitors and videotape. That the clergymen would return to the US without having seen seven of the people known to be among the captives caused worry back home that these captives may have been killed.

Which did not prevent the three clerics from paying little attention to the whispered pleas for help from a few of the hostages, and hints about their being treated appallingly, in spite of how the staged display might appear from the outside.

Instead, Coffin—as he met with small groups of hostages brought to him throughout the day "warned against the vice of 'self-pity,' and encouraged the captive Americans to sing along with him as he played the piano and led them in carols."[40]

Later in the day—before ending their trip with a visit to Khomeini, and reporting to the media that the hostages were in good shape—the clerics went to the foreign ministry building to see the three Americans held there against their will. Chargé D'Affaires Laingen, wrote to his wife, Penne, of the visit: "We found [them] sobered by the experience, clearly *surprised by the rigidity of the zealots holding the hostages* [emphasis added], and perhaps that is enough to make the trip worthwhile."[41]

Two days prior, Laingen had made the following entry in his journal: "I grieve at what this is doing to Islam's image among our people—and this during the year-long celebrations in the United States of the 14th century of Islam!..."[42]

What Laingen did not know when he wrote these words was that this would not be his or his staff's last Christmas in captivity. Nor did he know about another "unanticipated" bombshell about to explode in the face of the dialogue-seeking Carter administration.

The "Surprise" Invasion of Afghanistan

One of Carter's first goals after assuming office was to reach an understanding with the Soviet Union. Having witnessed the erosion of Détente practically from the moment it was toasted at the Kremlin in 1972, the president was determined to get things back on track. To this end, he was intent on conducting a second—and eventually a third—round of Strategic Arms Limitation Talks (SALT).

SALT I, between former President Richard Nixon and Soviet leader Leonid Brezhnev, had resulted in Détente, an agreement to curtail ballistic missiles. SALT II was going to focus on a mutual restriction of nuclear forces. SALT III would reduce nuclear weapons.

Indeed, in his first press conference as president, Carter had said:

"...We have the capability, as do the Soviets, to detect the launching of opposing missiles, and then I, as President, and the leaders in Russia would have to be faced with the question of how much of a retaliatory attack to make. But in the exchange, tens of millions of people would be killed. And the threat of this kind of holocaust is what makes it important that we do keep an adequate deterrent capability. And it also is crucial for all of us to remember that it is necessary to have drastic reduction in dependence on atomic weapons. Almost every major speech that I have made since I have been involved in national politics, I expressed—committed, first, to stabilize the situation; second, to have demonstrable reductions in dependence upon atomic weapons and set as our committed long-range goal complete elimination of nuclear weapons from the Earth..."[43]

What Carter didn't realize as he made these statements, however, was that it would take more than two years before Brezhnev would agree to meet with him. Instead, he was only given brief access to SR Foreign Minister Andrei Gromyko and Ambassador to the US Anatoli Dobrynin.

This did not prevent the US leader from going all out to woo his Soviet counterpart—just as he subsequently would court Khomeini—like a supplicant lover begging for a chance to prove himself worthy.

"I was able to send my second letter to Secretary General Brezhnev, much more substantive than the first," he wrote, a few days after his press conference. "I hope and believe that this exchange of confidential messages will lead to a better understanding between the Soviets and us. It's important that he understand the commitment I have to human rights preservation first of all, and secondly that he understand I'm sincere about my desire to reduce nuclear armaments. If he's willing to cooperate, we'll get something done before four years goes [sic] by."[44]

The two heads of state finally came face to face on June 15 in Vienna. Here they would clink their glasses to mark the signing of SALT II, which had been agreed upon the previous month. Carter "went to [the summit] visibly excited. He told aides that he had looked forward to meeting Brezhnev more than almost anything else during his years as President, and he spent an unprecedented amount of time preparing for the encounter."[45]

In the context of Carter's view of what has come to be called the "global community," this behavior was not surprising. As Norman Podhoretz described at the time, "The President or National Security Adviser, Zbigniew Bzezinski, might point in an extremity to Soviet misbehavior"—of which there was much and varied—"But in statement after statement by the President himself, his Secretary of State, his Ambassador to the UN, his leading expert on Soviet affairs, and his apologists in the universities and the press, the American people were told that the Soviet Union and the United States had, in Secretary Vance's phrase, 'similar dreams and aspirations,' and that the Soviets were pursuing the same objectives as we were—stability and peace."[46]

But what Brezhnev was *really* pursuing was Soviet military superiority. Any deal that would lead the Americans to curtail their own weapons' systems was worth entering into. His objectives were not "stability and peace," but rather world dominance through power. Furthermore, he couldn't stand Carter. While the US president may have thought that his human rights agenda would make him popular among his enemies, it actually had the opposite effect. And, as a key human-rights abuser, the Soviet Union did not take meddling into its internal affairs lightly. Brezhnev said as much in a private meeting with Carter at the American Embassy in Vienna, which Carter described as follows:

"...He referred to human rights, saying that the Soviet Union is not against this subject as a discussion on ideological grounds, but there is a problem if it is discussed as official state-to-state policy. There can be no progress if trade is related to human rights; they have not related trade to the unemployment rate in the United States, nor racial discrimination, nor the violation of the rights of women. This is a sensitive subject for the Soviets and not a legitimate ground for discussion between him and me."[47]

Though this meant no bargaining for the release of prisoners of Zion, such as Anatoly Sharansky, Carter continued to believe that the SR no longer need be contained and restrained. He also continued to hope that, with the right rapprochement between the two superpowers, the rest of the world would follow suit.

The US Congress wasn't so confident, and feared that SALT II would severely weaken American defense. In spite of the president's best efforts, they would not ratify the document he had signed with the Soviet secretary-general. Though frustrating to Carter at the time, it would turn out to be irrelevant. Come Christmas—a mere six months after the Carter-Brezhnev summit—the Soviets took advantage of the fact that the US was preoccupied with the hostage crisis to invade Afghanistan. In a swift move to take control, Soviet commandos assassinated Prime Minister Hafizullah Amin. The Soviet leadership immediately replaced him with Babrak Karmal—a leading Afghani Marxist who had been living in exile in the SR.

With a Soviet puppet government installed by way of a violent military attack against a country in the Persian Gulf, not only was it no longer feasible for Carter to continue on the SALT track, but now he was faced with an even bigger problem. Iran, which shared its northern border—1,250 miles long—with the Soviet Union, was no longer led by a US ally, thanks to Carter administration cooperation in the Shah's downfall. Instead, there was the Ayatollah Khomeini, gloating over the smooth and easy takeover of the US Embassy, with no repercussions.

Indeed, even the hoped-for economic sanctions were meeting resistance at the UN. As expected, the Soviets vetoed them. And the allies who had promised Vance they would support America started to backtrack on their original verbal assurances.

This prompted Ambassador McHenry, at an NSC meeting on December 28, to propose "a two-state process intended to break the negotiating stalemate. An immediate UN resolution would direct [UN] Secretary General [Kurt Waldheim]...to go to Iran to negotiate the release of the hostages. If he was unable to report progress within one week, sanctions would be imposed."[48]

But Waldheim was on a plane to Tehran before the Security Council even voted for the resolution, which would turn out to make little difference in the grander scheme of things, both within the UN and without.

On his arrival in Iran, Waldheim was received with verbal assaults by seething demonstrators; his car was surrounded by bloodthirsty mobs; the hostage-takers would not allow him into the embassy to see the captive American diplomats; and Khomeini refused to meet with him. This was to have been expected. Anti-Waldheim statements made by Khomeini and the hostage-takers were published in *The New York Times* and elsewhere on the eve of his trip. Nothing short of returning the Shah to face judgment, they said, would lead to the release of the hostages.

This did not weaken Carter's resolve to drum up support at the UN for sanctions—even though a Soviet veto would render any resolution meaningless. To complicate matters further, the Iranians were no more in favor of the Soviet invasion of Afghanistan than the Americans; and Carter's response to both enemies—the one for assaulting American sovereignty and the other American interests—was to beg other countries to help.

"I sent messages to our allies, key non-aligned leaders, plus all the Muslim countries—urging them to speak out strongly against the Soviet action and to share their thoughts about what should be done," he wrote. "I also sent on the Hot Line the sharpest message I have ever sent to Brezhnev, telling him that the invasion of Afghanistan would seriously and adversely affect the relationship between our two countries."[49]

By New Year's Eve, the situation was as follows: According to the new constitution in Iran, the Ayatollah Khomeini was now officially "Supreme Leader" for life. The hostages were still being brutalized and brainwashed, with no end to their plight in sight. The other countries of the Gulf were watching America capitulate, which weakened their desire to be allied with it. The Soviets were controlling Afghanistan. And Jimmy Carter and his wife, Rosalynn, "welcomed in" the year 1980 "by ourselves, which is the best way for us to do it."[50]

CHAPTER THREE

January 1980

As the New Year arrived, Carter was pleased to learn he was ahead of Kennedy in the polls. Whatever else was going on in the world, he had to keep his eye on getting reelected.

Meanwhile, in Iran, things weren't going so smoothly for him. As Bruce Laingen sat seething at the Foreign Ministry while watching a "documentary" aired on Iranian television about Christmas at the embassy,[51] Kurt Waldheim was being treated to a frightening and humiliating reception in the streets nearby. This was the day Laingen "felt bitterness in ways that I never have before."[52] It was also the point of realization for Waldheim of the powerlessness even of a position as internationally exalted as his own in post-Shah Iran.

Indeed, the veteran Viennese diplomat was so shocked by his treatment in the Islamic Republic that he returned to the US both visibly shaken and bearing Carter bad tidings: sanctions won't weaken the resolve of these people.

Muscle-flexing, Carter-style

But the president now had the invasion of Afghanistan on his mind, and what measures he was going to have to take in response. It troubled him deeply to table SALT II, after having been so proud of the "successful" outcome of his summit with Brezhnev. And suddenly here he was—forced to recall the US ambassador[53] and consider limiting grain sales to the Soviets because of their infractions. Worse than that, as far as he was concerned, was the question of withdrawing US participation in the upcoming summer Olympics, slated to be held in Moscow. On one hand, he believed that boycotting the event "would be the most severe blow to the Soviets." On the other, he felt that "only if many nations act in concert would it be a good idea."[54]

On January 4, Carter addressed the nation to discuss potential punitive steps. He also reiterated his dedication to diplomacy as a means of making the world a better place in general—and of persuading Iran to release the hostages and the Soviet Union to get out of Afghanistan in particular.

"History teaches, perhaps, very few clear lessons," he concluded. "But surely one such lesson learned by the world at great cost is that aggression, unopposed, becomes a contagious disease."

Nowhere in his speech did he mention opposing aggression through the use of American military power.

The following day, on January 5, a mass demonstration was held in Tehran to express support for the hostage-takers. One million Iranians marched through the streets screaming that nothing other than the return of the Shah for prosecution would be a basis for negotiating the release of the embassy staff. The public sentiment towards America was loud and clear: "We don't fear you; it's you who needs to fear us."

Back in Washington on January 6, Carter met with Waldheim, who had just returned from his disastrous trip. Given the UN Secretary-General's recounting of it, and his suggestion for how the US might handle the situation without sanctions (namely, by striking a deal involving investigating the Shah's crimes), it was apparent that the Iranian mob had been correct in its assessment of who was afraid of whom.

Still, just as was the case during the revolution that ousted the Shah and ushered in Khomeini, the groups who had united around the ayatollah were neither uniform nor really united. Parliamentary elections were about to be held, and candidates from every possible faction were competing for power. On January 7, bloody riots broke out in Tabriz between Khomeini loyalists and opposition factions.

Suddenly, the presence of Western media outlets—which the hostage-takers had been only too happy to exploit for their own propaganda purposes—had become a liability. The last thing that Khomeini's henchmen wanted was for the American public to be watching televised footage of internecine strife. As soon as coverage of the event went on the air outside of Iran, all foreign journalists were banished from Tabriz. A week later, they would be expelled from the country altogether for "biased" reporting aimed at undermining the revolution. Rather than fearing that this would make it harder for him to have some clue of what was going on at the besieged embassy, Carter was pleased. He called the turn of events "a good move toward resolution of the hostage question."[55] He did not explain why, though it is likely he preferred trusting the back-channel diplomacy he was conducting—with French and other middlemen through his chief of staff, Hamilton ("Ham") Jordan—to bring the hostage crisis to an end without the use of force.

Though the next day he was treated to a detailed description of the horrors that the hostages were enduring,[56] Carter had bigger fish to fry. He was now preparing the text of his upcoming State of the Union address. It was no easy task, considering the challenges he was confronting, among them his intention to boycott the Olympics, for which he feared much flak—and which he would come to consider one of the hardest decisions he would have to make as president.

The issue of reinstating a registry for the draft was also causing him grief. He had entered the White House determined to erase the Vietnam War stigma of his predecessors. He was confident in his ability to do things differently through peaceful means. Having to rethink the military, after all his effort to render it obsolete, was not only personally painful, however. As with any policy statement that whiffed even faintly of American power, this one was causing members of Carter's inner circle to be apoplectic. "We're having practically a rebellion from Stu [chief domestic policy adviser Stuart Eizenstat] and Fritz [Vice President Walter Mondale]"[57] on this issue, he wrote—though he made it clear he was only moving on *registration* for the draft, not on actually drafting anyone.

A New Doctrine?

On January 23, the president delivered the State of the Union Address for which he had been preparing so painstakingly. It was in this speech that he outlined what came to be called the "Carter Doctrine."

What made it so unusual as to being debated until today is that its content appeared to constitute a departure from the president's previous positions on how America should handle the current challenges to its national security. Though filled with the usual references to peace and human rights, it was a far cry from the "Malaise speech" he had given a mere six months earlier.

In that address, he said that the greatest threat to American democracy was "a crisis of confidence…that strikes at the very heart and soul and spirit of our national will," deriving from Americans' materialistic goals and indulgences.

And now here he was, indicating that there might be greater threats to the country than consumerism and "self-interest." Perhaps *actual* attacks on sovereignty and regional stability—committed by enemies not the least bit interested in American peace overtures—were of at least as much concern, if not more.

This is how he put it: "The implications of the Soviet invasion of Afghanistan could pose the most serious threat to the peace since the Second World War...But verbal condemnation is not enough. The Soviet Union must pay a concrete price for their aggression... Meeting this challenge will take national will, diplomatic and political wisdom, economic sacrifice, and, of course, *military capability* [emphasis added]. We must call on the best that is in us to preserve the security of this crucial region. Let our position be absolutely clear: an attempt by any outside force to gain control of the Persian Gulf region will be regarded as an assault on the vital interests of the United States of America, and such an assault will be repelled by any means necessary, *including military force* [emphasis added]."

As Podhoretz described it, this was "a new version, or so it seemed, of the Truman Doctrine of old. If the President could be believed, the period of strategic retreat was over and a new period of containment had begun."[58]

But could Carter, Podhoretz asked, be believed? And even if he could—which was not likely, given his convictions, the make-up of his cabinet, his continued reticence in relation to the hostage crisis, and his unfaltering faith in SALT II—was it too late to undo the damage?

Backchannel Diplomacy

While supporters and critics argued over the wisdom and integrity of Carter's supposed about-face, two indirectly connected things were going on behind the scenes, beyond America's borders. One involved secret meetings between two Carter administration officials, "Ham" Jordan and assistant secretary of state for Near Eastern and South Asian affairs Harold Saunders, and two French Ghotbzadeh loyalists, Christian Bourguet and Hector Villalon.

Enjoying his role as covert operative on behalf of his boss who was otherwise bogged down, Jordan spent much of his time with the two middlemen in Paris and other cities. To keep the whole thing as hush-hush as possible, the Americans donned disguises worthy of a spy movie. Frequently using aliases and wearing wigs and fake mustaches, they would arrive at various predetermined destinations for the purpose of negotiating a deal for the return of the hostages—one that would satisfy their captors.

There were two problems with this arrangement. One was that the Iranian demands continued to include acknowledging the Shah's crimes for the purpose of having him executed. Even Ghotbzadeh, a "moderate" who hated the United States and Soviet Union equally, took the position that if the Americans would simply murder the Shah by lethal injection or other "medical" means, the whole issue would resolve itself.

The other was that Ghotbzadeh, a candidate for the Islamic Republic's first presidential election held on January 25, lost to Finance Minister Abolhassan Bani-Sadr by a wide margin. It thus would not be long before he was fired from his position as foreign minister—which meant that his power to negotiate any deals on behalf of Khomeini was non-existent, at best.

Unlike the fruitless backchannel negotiations with the dubious

Frenchmen, the other behind-the-scenes event that was taking place at the end of January would come to happy light. It was an operation later dubbed the "Canadian caper."

Six American diplomats who had escaped capture on the day of the embassy siege—and holed up in the homes of Canadian Ambassador Ken Taylor and another member of his staff—were actually on a Swissair flight back to the US. Thanks to the efforts of the Canadian government—involving false identities and forged passports for the escapees, and a complicated operation to get them out of Iran—the half-dozen "lucky" ones landed safely on American soil. Once the mission was accomplished, the Canadian diplomats, too, evacuated their embassy, leaving the Islamic Republic behind for good. So as not to jeopardize the safety of the six Americans or the Canadians during the weeks prior to their leaving Iran, the US had kept mum about their whereabouts. Only months later would it be revealed that America and Canada had worked in cahoots to bring about the desired outcome.[59]

CHAPTER FOUR

February and March 1980

Though the weather in Washington may have been wintry, Carter thought he could see spring on the horizon. The reasons for this were twofold. First, the six Americans who had escaped Iran were given a joyous welcome home—cause, indeed, for celebration.

Secondly, messages he was receiving from Iran seemed to bode well for the hostages. Both Ghotbzadeh and Bani-Sadr—according to the French mediators—were supposedly on board about resolving the crisis as quickly as possible.

Furthermore, they assured Ham, who in turn assured Carter, the differences between the American and Iranian positions were "minor." That this was either purposeful misrepresentation or wishful thinking on the part of the middlemen would not become apparent to the US president until much later. But it does help to explain why he was moved to feel forgiveness towards his aggressors.

In his speech to the National Prayer Breakfast—an annual Washington gathering organized by the Fellowship Foundation and hosted by members of Congress—Carter stressed "the need to pray for our enemies, thank God for our trials and disappointments, and have in our hearts love for others..."[60]

Carter's "new" doctrine aside, the next few weeks saw a furious flurry of American diplomatic activity aimed at avoiding the use of military force in relation to the Soviet Union and Iran.

Indeed, the State Department was in overdrive, as was the UN Secretary-General. As officials worked on getting other countries behind punitive measures against the Soviet Union, Waldheim was by trying to come up with a solution to the impasse in the hostage crisis. This involved creating a commission that would investigate the Shah's crimes—and America's role in them—in exchange for the release of the embassy staff.

The two issues were not unrelated. In order to garner wide support against the Soviets, including in the Muslim world, America decided to hold off on its sanctions against Iran, not backed by many of its allies.

Moreover, because the Islamic Republic now had a new president— one whose candidacy had been backed by the currently ill ayatollah[61]— the administration harbored hope was that this was an opportunity to make a deal with someone who actually had the authority to do so. A trade ban, it was felt, "would produce further ammunition for the militants to wage their anti-American campaign,"[62] and might jeopardize efforts to negotiate with Bani-Sadr.

Still, the "government" in Iran at this point was being run by the Revolutionary Council, a temporary arrangement until elections for the parliament (Majlis), slated to take place in March.

Meanwhile, Jordan's meetings with Villalon and Bourget continued. More importantly, they arranged for him to have a face-to-face with Ghotbzadeh. As had been the case every time Carter authorized Ham to agree to conditions set out by the Iranian "representative," the ante was upped.

Carter still believed that serious progress was being made. On February 11, Carter wrote the following entry in his diary: "Cy, Ham and [Assistant Secretary of State] Hal Saunders had a good meeting with Waldheim, settled on members of the Iran commission, and *got positive reports from Iran* [emphasis added]. Kurt will issue his statement tonight, and the Iranians will respond that they accept the commission, which will go there within a week. There will be no interrogation of hostages. The hostages will be removed to a hospital, and a report will be made by the commission to the UN and published. Then the hostages will be released, and Bani-Sadr will make statements as agreed ahead of time."

It seemed that it was just a matter of ironing out the final details before the hostages would be home with their families. Reports in the foreign media hinted that this was the case, as well. These were based on statements made by Bani-Sadr to the effect that Iran would accept a UN commission, and once it determined that the Shah had committed war crimes with the aid of the United States, the hostages would be transferred to the care of the Revolutionary Council, prior to being released.

Since the Revolutionary Council's days were numbered, it sounded as though the most the hostages would have to remain in captivity would be another few weeks.

It was then that Carter "decided not to initiate a rescue mission for the hostages...and to terminate... [the] Iran covert operation, since we are satisfied with Bani-Sadr until now."[63]

While Carter may have been satisfied with Bani-Sadr, Ghotbzadeh was anything but. When Jordan returned from his tête-à-tête with the (soon-to-be-ousted) foreign minister, he reported as much in writing. Included in his summary to the president was Ghotbzadeh's request that the US assassinate the Shah. Carter's heart sank. Things were not proceeding as smoothly as he had hoped, after all. It was especially frustrating not knowing whose statements to trust.

What Carter did learn, however, was that the hostage-takers—when asked whether they would accept Bani-Sadr's deal with Waldheim if the Revolutionary Council were to demand they release the embassy staff—said they would only take orders from the ayatollah himself. Yet, the one authority who had remained mum throughout this period was Khomeini.

Then, when the Supreme Leader finally *did* open his mouth, what came out was a dismissal of every agreement that had been reached on the UN commission and release of the hostages. Most disturbing was a statement he released announcing that only after the new parliament was formed—which could take until April at the earliest—would the issue even be discussed. The new Islamic Assembly, he declared, would decide under what terms the hostages would be freed.

"The Moslem and combatant students who occupied the den of espionage have by their revolutionary deed dealt a crushing body-blow against the world-devouring United States and have thereby made the nation proud," he said in an address to the Iranian public. "But since in the near future the representatives of the people will meet at the Islamic Consultative Assembly, the issue of the hostages will be up to the representatives of the people."[64]

That he issued this statement on the day before the arrival of the "agreed-upon" UN commission[65] was cause for great celebration among the captors at the embassy. It did not bode well, however, for the United States.

1980 was a leap year, which meant that the month of February—during which the hostages were not only bound and terrorized, but freezing as well—had 29 days. Metaphorically, it meant taking an even greater leap of faith than before about any deal involving their release.

As was to be expected, given the timing of Khomeini's statement and the response of the hostage-takers to it, when the UN commission members arrived in Tehran, they were not allowed into the besieged embassy. Instead, for more than two weeks they were treated to what Mark Bowden describes as the "graveyard and cripple tour" of SAVAK cruelty and Shah criminality.

Sixteen days later, they left the country without even having seen how the hostages were faring. On March 11, the American public watched the televised scene of the UN emissaries boarding a plane out of Tehran in dismay. The hostages' families realized that their dream for a swift resolution to their loved-ones' fate at this point was no more than the same old nightmare.

When the panel landed in Zurich on its way to New York to report back to Waldheim, its Algerian co-chairman, Mohamed Bedjaoui, told reporters the mission "was not a failure, but of course we are disappointed. It was a step on the road. But it was not a failure."[66]

To add irony to idiocy, back in Iran, Bani-Sadr was doing what appeared to the American president to be a political about-face—due to "weakness." In fact, he was merely doing what he had always done, which is to secure his own power base and look out for Number One. Indeed, even while the UN commission was in Iran—a move supposedly backed by the new Iranian president—Bani-Sadr was standing with the "students" on top of one of the guardhouses of the US Embassy making a speech to mark the end of "National Mobilization Week." His speech was followed by an anti-American diatribe delivered by one of the participants.[67]

It should not have been surprising, then, when the very same Bani-Sadr, who had accused the hostage-takers of being "Communists and Zionists" in early February, suddenly changed his tune when the UN Commission exited Iran. At this point, he began praising the radicals as "patriots" and saying that if anybody—mainly the "naïve" Americans—

had thought that he was some kind of "moderate," they had another think coming.

Carter's response was to send Bani-Sadr a "tough message" (Carter's words) reiterating US demands: "release of American hostages unharmed and quickly; *normal relations with Iran when the Iranian government desires this; recognizing the fact of the revolution; and an opportunity for Iran to air its grievances, either in the UN, the International Court of Justice, or through the world press* [emphasis added]."[68]

In this message—which Bani-Sadr received on March 27—Carter also set a deadline: If, by March 31, the hostages were not transferred to the control of the Iranian government, the US would take "additional *non-belligerent* measures that we have withheld until now [emphasis added]."[69] According to the NSC's Gary Sick, "The United States had already taken most of the steps available to it to punish Iran politically, diplomatically and economically, so the list of [additional non-belligerent measures] was not particularly long or fearsome." This caused a reporter to ask Sick a sarcastic question: "When are you going to unsheathe your wet noodle?"[70]

It was a reasonable taunt, given the lengthy and ongoing assault not only against dozens of American diplomats individually, but against America itself. This fact did not prevent Secretary of State Vance from insisting that Carter not make good on his word when the deadline arrived and the hostages were no closer to being released than before.

But since, on that day, Washington received a message that Bani-Sadr had met with the "student leaders," and would give a speech on April 1 detailing the results of that meeting, Vance begged Carter to wait a little longer. What's another day or two in the larger scheme of things—Vance argued—considering how dedicated Ghotbzadeh and Bani-Sadr were to resolving the crisis?

Carter wasn't too happy. He had written a "tough" memo to Bani-

Sadr threatening more sanctions if his conditions weren't met by the last day in March. And now he felt that giving the Iranians more time would make him look weak. But he gave in to Vance, nevertheless.

None of this made it into his diary. His entry for March 31 dealt, instead, with financial reform legislation, "a landmark law, which completely revises the handling of deposits, the paying of interest, and the management of commercial banks, savings and loans, credit institutions of all kinds."

Delta's Missed Opportunity

As February and March came and went, so, too, did Delta Force's opportunity to take advantage of the perfect weather conditions for the rescue operation dubbed "Eagle Claw."

"The news photographs for that period showed the armed guards [at the embassy] spending a lot of time warming themselves around fires they'd laid in 55-gallon drums," wrote Commander Beckwith. "It was cold in Tehran. When a guard's cold he is less alert. He has other things on his mind; his bed, his woman, a hot meal. He doesn't want to waste another freezing night, stomping his feet to keep warm, shuffling monotonously up and down the deserted, windswept streets around the embassy. This was good for the planned mission. It was better to go into Iran when the weather conditions favored us rather than them."[71]

Catching the enemy when he was cold was only a minor part of the time-frame consideration, however.

LTG (Ret.) William (Jerry) Boykin, a founding member and subsequent commander of Delta Force who participated in Eagle Claw, explained it to me as follows: "We needed X number of hours of darkness in order to pull this complex, two-day operation off. We had to get into

Iran, refuel, and get into a hive site, all under the cover of darkness. The next night, we would then have to go in, rescue the hostages and get out again, also under the cover of darkness. We told Carter that, due to the days growing longer as winter turned to spring, there would be a point at which we would no longer have the necessary number of hours of darkness. I believe we determined that April 30 would be the very last day such an operation could even be attempted. And we stressed that the longer we waited, the more we would be cutting into our margin for error. But he kept delaying and delaying—relying on the diplomatic process and listening to the objections of Cyrus Vance..."[72]

Having no choice but to wait for an OK from the political echelon to execute Eagle Claw was, in itself, stressful for Beckwith and his men—among them Boykin. But it was particularly anxiety-producing, given the experience of the months leading up to it.

Boykin shook his head in disgust as he recalled a visit by Stansfeld Turner to "The Farm"—a military training reservation in Virginia—where Delta Force was preparing for Eagle Claw.

"He came to see us, and insisted that he wanted to be of assistance in any way possible. 'How can I help?' he asked. We said that we needed to know exactly where the hostages were being held in the 27-acre compound of the embassy, and how many were in each building. 'Oh, um...,' he answered sheepishly. This was the one thing the head of the CIA couldn't offer—thanks to his purposely having reduced the human intelligence capabilities of his organization to the barest minimum."

Another thing Delta needed was ground transportation in Iran to deliver the rescuers from the landing point in the desert to the embassy. This, too, required having CIA operatives on the ground. As Boykin told it, "They actually had to approach a guy in Germany who had been among those retired from the CIA, bring him back on active duty, and get him to go into Iran to buy trucks for us."

In spite of not really believing that they would ever actually be called upon by the current administration to conduct a mission, Delta Force trained tirelessly, making sure to be prepared at a moment's notice. This training involved, among other things, practicing a rescue operation in an area built to replicate that of the US Embassy in Tehran in as much detail as possible. Scaling the model embassy walls was by no means the only form of intense physical rehearsal that the men chosen for the mission spent their time perfecting. But it was a major one, as was practicing the taking out of the guards, the locating of the hostages and the evacuating of them to a nearby soccer stadium where they would be scooped up by helicopters.

"Not again!" the men would wail under their breath each time they were told to repeat the whole exercise from beginning to end. This was not for lack of taking their mission seriously. On the contrary, said Boykin, "We trained with intensity and passion and great hope, but not with expectations. As the months went on, we reached the point at which we didn't believe that Carter would launch the operation. He had said upfront, at the very beginning of the embassy takeover: 'We will do nothing to jeopardize the lives of those hostages,' when what he should have said was: 'We'd like to resolve this without a military conflict, but make no mistake: all options are on the table.'"

Chapter Five

April 1980

On the morning of April 1, as the Carter administration eagerly awaited to hear what President Bani-Sadr would say about the fate of the hostages, the Iranian public was attending a mass rally to commemorate the first anniversary of the establishment of the Islamic Republic.

At the rally, held at Freedom Square in Tehran, there were two key speakers. One was Khomeini's son, Hojatloislam Ahmad Khomeini, who delivered a statement on behalf of his father; the other was Bani-Sadr.

Khomeini's speech was full of the usual anti-American vitriol. Referring to Carter as the "Great Satan," he accused the US president of cheating him for pernicious purposes. "By expressions of moderation and flattery, he is trying to pull the wool over our eyes and to win his political gamble against his rivals by playing a trick on our nation," Khomeini asserted. This was apparently a reference to Carter's repeated conciliatory statements and gestures towards him and the Islamic Republic—which the ayatollah wasn't buying. He wanted the Shah's head delivered to him on a platter; he wanted the US to accept blame for all of Iran's past ills and current hostage stalemate.

"Threatening with military occupation and landing paratroopers in the den of espionage and threatening economic blockade and isolation of the country and having failed to achieve anything, he has now embarked upon a political plot and a satanic conspiracy," Khomeini declared, adding: "Mr. Carter must realize that by sending the deposed Shah to Egypt and apologizing for past mistakes, by admitting American treacheries against oppressed nations, including Iran, and then asking me, as a member of the great Iranian nation, to find a solution for the espionage den, he is following the wrong path... By delivering the deposed Shah, this enemy of Islam and Iran, to the enemy [Anwar Sadat of Egypt] who has deeply hurt the world's Moslems by his shameful deeds, he has further complicated the way to a solution."[73]

Bani-Sadr's speech—which lasted a full two hours, and only included a brief discussion of the hostage situation—put the ball back in Carter's court. Rather than responding to the warnings of the US president about measures he would take if the hostages were not handed over to the Revolutionary Council and subsequently released, the Iranian president laid out his own government's conditions for a resolution to the crisis.

"If the American authorities make an official announcement that they will not make any propaganda or say any words or make any provocative acts about the hostages until the formation of the parliament, then the Revolutionary Council will accept the control of the hostages,"[74] he declared.

Due to the time difference between Tehran and Washington—and the time needed to have the above speeches translated into English— Carter and his men were in the Oval Office for a pre-Bani-Sadr-speech strategy meeting at the crack of dawn. In attendance at the gathering were Secretary of State Vance, Deputy Secretary of State Warren Christopher, National Security advisor Brzezinski, Assistant Secretary of State for Near Eastern Affairs Saunders, advisor David Aaron, Chief of Staff Ham Jordan, Press Secretary Jody Powell, and NSC staffer Gary Sick.

Putting their heads together to come up with the right wording of the statement they would release to the press following Bani-Sadr's speech, the men argued over the nuances of phrases, so as not to upset the Iranian regime any further. They also discussed the potential consequences, at home and abroad, of not imposing additional sanctions on the Islamic Republic.

When the meeting ended, Jody Powell made a quick statement to reporters about Bani-Sadr's speech. An hour later, Carter held a slightly longer news conference in the Oval Office. In it, he stated that the US would be giving the Iranians more time to work out a solution.

"...This morning, the President of Iran has announced that the hostages' control will be transferred to the government of Iran, which we consider to be a positive step," he said. "In light of that action, we did not consider it appropriate now to impose additional sanctions..."[75]

As Carter delivered his message—at 7:20 a.m.—polls for the democratic primary were opening up in Wisconsin and Kansas. White House staffers admitted that the timing was not coincidental. They told reporters that they hoped his comments on Iran would work to his advantage.

But Carter was nervous, and rightly so, which is why he did not reveal everything about Bani-Sadr's speech that he could or should have. He purposely did not mention that the Iranian president had made the transfer of the hostages conditional upon US promises not to say or do anything "provocative." He knew this wouldn't go over well, particularly on the heels of a US ultimatum to Iran which he did not carry out. He also realized at this point that his handling of the hostage crisis was going to constitute a key factor in his electoral popularity.

True, during the period immediately following the embassy takeover, the public had rallied behind him. Pressure on him not to act too hastily or aggressively, particularly from the families of the hostages, was high; his succumbing to it was perceived originally not as weakness, but rather as the responsible lesser of two evils.

But by April—six months into the crisis—the American people's patience was running thin. When the UN commission to Iran had returned not only empty-handed, but without having even seen the hostages, sentiment across the US shifted. It was one thing to exercise caution in this delicate situation. It was quite another for the leader of a superpower to behave as if he had no red lines beyond which attacks against his nation could not go. Imposing additional sanctions didn't sound like such a threat; postponing the move for a second time, based on what by now was clearly wishful thinking, was certain to raise eyebrows, if not ire.

Taking the Decision

The public was not Carter's only concern, however. Keeping his inner circle on board with his policies was also a challenge. Indeed, every time a discussion of a raid to rescue the hostages came up, Cy Vance threatened to resign. Anything that might lead to the spilling of any blood was abhorrent to him, and he made no bones about it. His deputy, Warren Christopher—who increasingly replaced him in meetings when he announced he wouldn't pursue a second term after the November election—wasn't much different.

Indeed, it was Christopher who blanched during a meeting on April 16, when Col. Beckwith described in detail how Delta force would perform a rescue operation if given the green light to do so. When Beckwith got to the part about scaling the embassy walls and "taking out the guards," Christopher stopped him in mid-sentence.

"What do you mean?" he asked Beckwith. "Will you shoot them in the shoulder or what?"

"No Sir," Beckwith replied respectfully. "We're going to shoot each of them twice, right between the eyes."

"You mean you're really going to shoot to kill?" Christopher responded. "You really are?"[76]

That meeting took place just under two weeks after Carter had sent another message to Bani-Sadr—this one stating that the US was running out of alternatives to its previous warnings about taking stricter measures against Iran. Days had passed since the American president had agreed to hold off on additional sanctions, to give his Iranian counterpart more time to maneuver. But to no avail.

Again, Iran tried to stall, this time by requesting a clarification of the message.

April 6 was Easter Sunday. Its significance was lost on no one; another holiday was passing with the hostages still in captivity.

On April 7, Carter met with the NSC to discuss the fact that negotiations for the release of the hostages weren't working, after all—due, he believed, to internecine Iranian power struggles.

The upshot was a decision to "break diplomatic relations [with Iran]; expel all Iranian diplomats; declare an embargo against shipment of any goods to Iran except food and medicine; make a census of claims against Iranian assets [held in the US]; and expedite through legislation a conclusion of those claims."[77] At this point, he also raised the Delta Force rescue operation as a real possibility.

Winds of a Different War

Meanwhile, age-old tensions were heating up along Iran's border with Iraq. Iraqi dictator Saddam Hussein's secular Baathist regime adhered to Arab nationalism. The Ayatollah Khomeini—who had even announced that he "felt nothing" about returning to his native Iran after years of exile—was a pan-Islamist. Iraq had a Sunni majority, Iran a Shi'ite one.

Still, out of a shared hatred of the deposed Shah, Saddam had openly supported the Iranian Revolution, and called upon Khomeini to drop the hatchet. But Khomeini wasn't interested in a truce with what he considered to be an un-Islamic regime—one which he accused of being an American puppet. He wanted all Shi'ites in the Arab world to do what he had done in Iran: rise up against the leaders of their respective countries. With his support, Iraqi Shi'ites did just that, launching a violent campaign against Saddam. Indeed, during the month of April, as Carter was imposing new restrictions on Iran—and gearing up towards a potential rescue mission—twenty officials in Saddam's government were murdered by Iraqi militants. Even Saddam's Deputy Prime Minister and Information Minister were the targets of attempted assassination.

Saddam was not only livid; he was scared that he and his regime would be under serious threat if he didn't stomp out this dangerous internal rebellion. So he went on the offensive. On April 9, he executed a prominent Iraqi Shi'ite cleric and his activist sister.[78] Their hangings caused ripples throughout the Islamic world.

The following day, on April 10, the hostage-takers at the embassy in Tehran issued what Carter referred to as "all kinds of crazy threats."[79] These were that they would kill all their captives if Iraq were to invade Iran—or if the US were to attempt a military operation.

Iraq wouldn't invade Iran until six months later. Operation Eagle Claw, on the other hand, was undertaken within two weeks.

Disaster in the Desert

On April 24, Beckwith and the dozens of military personnel who had been training for months, took off for Desert One—the designated spot in Iran, about 200 miles southeast of Tehran. The day they had been waiting for had finally arrived, and they were anxious. Before setting out, they gathered together and bowed their heads.

"Almighty God, we've placed ourselves in your hands," said Boykin, who led the men in prayer. "And we ask you to lead us and guide us so that we might liberate our fellow Americans. We ask for you hand of mercy to be upon us. We ask for wisdom and strength and courage. We ask you to keep us safe, and to keep safe the people we're going after. Bring us all home to our families. And I pray this in Christ's name. Amen."[80] After that, they sang the national anthem, grabbed their gear and entered the plane that was to transport them to the first leg of their final destination.

They had all grown beards for the occasion, and donned blue jeans and black jackets with no visible American markings. Their dog tags were hidden under their shirts. Each had a small US flag sewn on his sleeve, covered by a Velcro patch, to be removed when encountering the hostages. This would be Delta's way of telling the captives that they were being saved by their countrymen.

It never got to that.

Due to a sand cloud, one of the eight designated helicopters crash landed, and another returned to the aircraft carrier, the USS Nimitz, stationed in the Indian Ocean. Beckwith had made it clear that the absolute minimum number of helicopters required for the operation was six; having more than two in reserve was impossible, due to limited space on the aircraft carrier.

But one of the remaining six that did make it to Desert One had been seriously damaged in the sand cloud, making it inoperable. There was no choice, then, but for Beckwith—with Carter's consent—to abort the mission.

As if this weren't unfortunate enough for all concerned, as soon as the men began to head for home, one of the helicopters crashed into one of the transport planes. Suddenly, Desert One was lit up like Las Vegas on the Fourth of July, rather than shrouded in darkness. Fireballs from the collision exploded into the night sky. Trapped in the blazing aircraft, eight of the men perished. Their distraught comrades-in-arms had no recourse but to hightail it out of the area as fast as they could.

Not only had the rescue mission been thwarted. But the corpses of dedicated American servicemen were left behind, along with the burnt aircraft—vestiges of the top-secret endeavor that would be exposed at sunrise for the Iranian regime to see and gloat over.

Early Mourning

By the time Americans arose in the morning, the whole operation—about which there had been much media speculation, but no actual knowledge—was over and done with. At 7 a.m., President Carter took to the airways to make a statement about the events of the past several hours. The mood in the country, already low, moved to one of genuine demoralization—not the "malaise" Carter had insisted the nation was suffering from, but rather a distress of a very different nature. The US already looked weak and helpless as a result of inaction following the embassy takeover; now it would be a complete laughing stock. And the hostages would be at greater peril than ever before.

The next day, on April 26, Carter met with his top advisers to give a post mortem on Eagle Claw, and begin discussing the possibility of an additional rescue mission. No mention seemed to have been made of the fact that two major factors would make this well nigh impossible: that the US had lost the element of surprise against Iran, and that the deadline for having enough hours of darkness in a 24-hour period had just passed.

On April 27, Carter and others, including Vance, took a secret trip to visit Beckwith and representatives from all the squadrons who had participated in the failed mission. During the flight, Vance—who had opposed the rescue operation in the first place—told Carter he was submitting his resignation, to be effective the following day. Carter agreed. When he returned to the White House, after "an inspirational and thrilling meeting with the rescue team,"[81] he told Secretary of Defense Brown that his first choice to replace Vance was Senator Ed Muskie. Brown concurred that it was a good choice.

The following day, on April 28, Muskie agreed to take the job. He, like everyone else in the administration at this moment, had his work cut out for him. For one thing, as the new guy on the diplomatic block, he was going to have to forge ties with America's allies to get the additional sanctions against Iran back on track. For another, he was going to have to learn about and take charge of US diplomacy while his boss was by stepping up his campaigning efforts—now more uphill than ever.

Allah and the Ayatollah

While Americans mourned the loss of the servicemen and feared for the lives of the hostages, Iranians celebrated victory over the Great Satan. Allah, they believed, had intervened on their behalf. The remains of the burnt planes and corpses in the Iranian desert were proof to them that the God of Islam was on their side against the non-Muslim world. Heads

and other scorched body parts were proudly displayed at a press conference held at the embassy, to flaunt Iran's victory over the superpower it
had brought to its knees.

To express their elation, tens of thousands of Iranians took to the
rooftops in the days following America's "folly" to chant *"allahu akbar!"*
at the top of their lungs.

For his part, Khomeini—along with Bani-Sadr and Ghotbzadeh—
milked the situation for all it was worth. The ayatollah warned that
any additional attacks would result in the immediate execution of the
hostages. Bani-Sadr and Ghotbzadeh accused Carter of committing an
act of war that violated international law.

This was the only "silver lining" in the cloud that hung over families
of the hostages. Rather than making good on his original threat, Khomeini was now conveying the message that this would not happen until
the "next time."

Meanwhile, the hostage-takers—though buoyed by the failure of the
rescue mission—decided, nevertheless, to take further precautions. One
was to reinforce the gates of the embassy with sandbags and additional
guards. Another was to prepare to disperse the hostages in different
locations throughout the country. It had become clear that holding all of
their captives in one place (save the three held at the Foreign Ministry)
was not so wise. Allah and the ayatollah's support aside, there were still
the day-to-day details to consider, among them the possibility that the
Great Satan was not done attempting to get his people back.

Unlike the crowds screaming with jubilance beyond the confines
of the embassy, the hostages had no idea about the failed attempt to
rescue them. They did, however, sense that something was up. Their
guards seemed to be buzzing around more than usual, carrying greater
quantities of arms. What could it mean? Perhaps, one speculated, the
Islamic Republic was undergoing a coup.

When told to get ready to be moved, they knew one thing—that they weren't headed towards an interim stop on their way to freedom, but rather to a new phase of their interminable captivity.

Each grew more terrified as he or she was taken out, blindfolded, and transported in various vehicles, including small planes, to destinations outside of Tehran. Now, in addition to living in the terror and uncertainty to which they were growing unhappily accustomed, they were going to have to contend with their plight far away from each other and from the familiar surroundings of the embassy compound. It was in this fashion that they would spend the rest of their incarceration in a hostile land, with no sense of when—or if—they would ever see their homes again.

CHAPTER SIX

May, June, and July 1980

As spring descended on Washington—with the sunlit monuments of America's forefathers contrasting the pall cast over the White House—Carter turned his attentions to the issues over which he believed he had a modicum of control. It appeared that nothing he could do was going to have an impact on the internal politics of Iran, and no external pressure was working towards the release of the hostages. Maybe there was something he could do to defeat Teddy Kennedy in the Democratic Presidential primaries. It was to this goal that he devoted himself for the weeks following Eagle Claw.

Contending that the circumstances which had kept him in the capital area since the embassy seizure six months earlier "had been alleviated to some degree," he announced that he would lift his self-imposed ban on travel and campaigning and visit other parts of the country.[82]

It is unclear that the circumstances surrounding Iran had been "alleviated" at all—other than the fact that the hostages had not been executed when it was feared they would be.

In fact, if anything, the situation was worse than before. The conditions for another rescue operation could not be met; the hostages were now dispersed in unknown locations; the Iranian parliament, the Majlis—supposedly Carter's last hope—had yet to be established; and the most radical of the political factions in Iran were garnering the most support. It was they, after all, who had brought the Great Satan to its knees. It was just as Khomeini had said at the outset: "There's not a damned thing Carter can do about it."

Copycat Siege

Just as the US president was resigning himself to the scenario still unfolding in the Islamic Republic, another diplomatic mission was besieged—this one in Britain.

On the evening of April 30, six armed gunmen entered the Iranian Embassy in London and took its occupants hostage. The aggressors were members of the Arab minority in the Khuzestan province of Iran (which they referred to as Arabstan), assisted by Iraqi forces trying to create internecine strife for their enemy neighbor.

After taking 26 people hostage, they demanded that all Arab prisoners in jails in their province be released, and that they be given safe passage out of Britain. Both demands were denied, but negotiations resulted in the releases of five of the hostages.

The siege lasted five days. It ended on May 5, when the British sent commandos in to attack and rescue, after a hostage was killed and tossed out of the embassy. When the 17-minute raid was over, all but one of the hostages was rescued and five out of six of the hostage-takers were dead. The sixth was imprisoned for the next 27 years.

The tragic irony was not missed by anyone other than the regime in

Iran, which insisted that the siege against its embassy bore no resemblance to the one still in progress on its own soil.

British Prime Minister Margaret Thatcher, in an address before the House of Commons, took the opportunity to express hope that the siege and its outcome would lead to the release of the American hostages in Iran. Iranian officials balked at the suggestion. "The situations are completely different," they asserted, claiming that while the siege on their embassy in London was "an act of terrorism," the one going on in Iran was "a legitimate outcry against 25 years of oppression."[83]

The comparison was mind-boggling. If the situations were different, it was because of two main factors. One was that the Iranian embassy in London was protected by the British government, while the US embassy in Tehran was overtaken with the consent of the Iranian powers-that-be. Another was the amount of time it took for the Iranian embassy drama to be dealt with—a mere five days—relative to that underway in the Islamic Republic, six months and counting.

That Bani-Sadr's praise of the British government for putting a swift end to the aggression against its diplomats was the height of hypocrisy was clear to the American public. Less clear is how Carter viewed the episode, which did not make it into his diary.

What did was a brief description of "a moving, emotional ceremony at Arlington National Cemetery for the eight servicemen who died in the Iranian desert." Of this Carter wrote, "The families were more solicitous about my feeling than about their own sorrow."[84] This was apparently comforting to a president whose reelection was questionable, with polls showing that the American people were fed up with his fumbling on the hostage crisis and still reeling from Thatcher's handling of the Iranian embassy takeover.[85]

That was how a self-respecting nation should treat terrorists—quickly and unequivocally. No negotiation. No hesitation. No apologies.

'Crimes of America'

On May 31—the day that CNN was launched by Ted Turner and broadcast worldwide—the Majlis opened in Tehran with great fanfare. If this is what Carter had been anticipating as a way to get negotiations with Iran "back" on track, he was to be severely disappointed. At the ceremonial opening session, Khomeini gave a long rant about why Iranians must be better Islamists or suffer the consequences. And representatives of the Students Following the Line of the Iman (the hostage-takers) made a plea that the government not act out of fear of the Great Satan while dealing with the hostage issue.

It was obvious that the International Court of Justice ruling of the previous week hadn't made a dent in the Iranian position. According to the court's judgment—released on May 24—"...Iran has violated and is still violating obligations owed by it to the United States; ...these violations engage Iran's responsibility;...the Government of Iran must immediately release the United States nationals held as hostages and place the premises of the Embassy in the hands of the protecting power; ...no member of the United States diplomatic or consular staff may be kept in Iran to be subjected to any form of judicial proceedings or to participate in them as a witness; ...Iran is under an obligation to make reparation for the injury caused to the United States; and ...the form and amount of such reparation, failing agreement between the parties, shall be settled by the Court."[86]

Not only did the Iranian government ignore the verdict, but Bani-Sadr was by preparing for a special anti-United States event that was to take place on June 2 at the Tehran Hilton—re-dubbed the "Freedom Hotel"—for the occasion.

In attendance at the "Crimes of America Conference" were hundreds of participants from dozens of countries, among them the US.

Indeed, in spite of the Carter's imposed travel ban to the Islamic Republic, Ramsey Clark—who, six months earlier, had been denied entry into Iran as the president's emissary—took it upon himself to attend the current conference of his own volition. With the assistance of the Iranian delegation to the UN, he took with him a cast of radical characters, such as John Walsh and Charles Kimball (the clergymen who had visited the hostages over Christmas), Paul Washington, a civil rights activist, and George Wald, a Nobel Prize winner at Harvard famous for his left-wing views.[87]

At the event, Clark said he "could understand the seizure of the hostages in human terms," and defended the Iranian revolution. He also called for the release of the hostages on the grounds that their continued detention was harming Iranian interests. After his speech, he had a private meeting with Bani-Sadr, hoping to get some mention of the release of the hostages included in the conference resolutions.

None of this made him more popular with his hosts, however. On the contrary, he was accused of "plotting like a latter-day Rudolf Hess."[88]

In many ways, this was reminiscent of his treatment the first time around. As hard as he may have tried to persuade Khomeini and the others of his being a trustworthy and sympathetic middleman for their cause, he was no more to them but a pawn on the one hand and a spy for the Great Satan on the other. It was undoubtedly impossible for the Iranian strongmen to conceive of someone being that disloyal to his president and country; in their eyes, he *had* to have been speaking on behalf of Carter—for underhanded reasons, of course.

As a result, he returned home with nothing to show for his visit—and absolutely no progress whatsoever on the hostage front.

Though there was talk in the State Department about investigating and possibly prosecuting Clark for his violation of the travel ban, he and his entourage emerged from the whole episode unscathed.

And Then There Were 52

About a month after the "Crimes of America Conference," one of the US diplomats was released from captivity. This had nothing to do with efforts from Washington, however. It was, rather, the result of the hostage-takers' assessment that it would be better to get rid of the embassy's ailing vice consul while he was still alive.

Richard Queen, nearly 29 at the time, had grown increasingly physically disabled with each passing day of his incarceration. He experienced dizzy spells and partial paralysis of one side of his body. Neither the doctors who saw him at the embassy, nor the hospital in Tehran, could figure out what was the matter with him. He was diagnosed as having a "twisted spine."

When he was released on what Khomeini called "humanitarian grounds," he was flown to a hospital in Switzerland and then to Lindsay Air Force Base in Germany, where it was determined that he was suffering from multiple sclerosis.

His return to America was cause for great celebration and renewed hope that the other hostages might not be far behind. But to no avail. Another holiday had come and gone. This one, Independence Day, had an even more bitter-sweet symbolism than its predecessors. Indeed, the hostages were not at home celebrating freedom over hot dogs and beer. They were scattered across a foreign land, oppressed by their jailers—and now by the harsh Iranian summer heat, as well.

Carter was asked about their plight and his plans for resolving the crisis during a Merced, California town meeting he attended on the Fourth of July.

"...How to get the hostages home I've not yet discovered," he said. "But I hope that every American, every day, will remember those 53 hostages, remember them in our prayers. And I believe that they will be coming home safely."

Then, invoking Independence Day, he added, "It's not a sign of weakness that a great nation like ours has been so deeply concerned about this issue. Many countries in the world would forget about 53 people. They're not famous people; they're not great people, as far as their past accomplishments are concerned. They're just common, ordinary, good, dedicated, patriotic Americans. We have never forgotten them. And when 220 million Americans are deeply obsessed with the lives and safety of just 53 people for months, to me that's a sign of greatness."[89]

In keeping with his feeling that he was merely one of many Americans who hadn't "forgotten" the hostages—rather than the only one with the power actually to influence their fate—he, like the audience he was addressing, had no idea that within two weeks he would be hearing Queen's first-hand account of his and his fellow diplomats' torturous ordeal.

Less surprising than Queen's release, but equally unexpected, was another event later in the month that raised a new set of questions, if not false hopes, about the possibility of the release of the remaining hostages. On July 27, the Shah finally succumbed to his cancer and died in Cairo, his last place of refuge.

Cautious Optimism

If Pahlevi's return to Iran for prosecution and execution was no longer an issue, would the United States be able to persuade the regime in Tehran to release the hostages? Washington knew better by now than to count any chickens with regard to the Islamic Republic. Not only had repeated negotiations that seemed to be on the verge of a breakthrough not pan out, but it still wasn't clear to the president's men who, other than the Supreme Leader, was authorized to make deals. Furthermore, Khomeini's anti-American rhetoric was a fiery as ever.

Still, with the Shah out of the picture, the Majlis convening and the establishment of a cabinet supposedly happening any week now, it appeared that something in the landscape was shifting. It was this kind of movement that Carter—plum out of ideas as to how to extricate his diplomatic staff from their imprisonment—had been relying on while campaigning to win the democratic primaries.

Another factor that caused speculation in the White House about the possibility that the Islamic fundamentalists in Iran—who were garnering far more support than the likes of the more "moderate" Bani-Sadr—would be willing to resolve the hostage crisis in the near future was the Ramadan holiday. Some officials in Washington hoped that the ayatollahs would take the religious opportunity to release the hostages, since it was common for Muslim governments to award amnesties at the end of the month of fasting.

But others weren't so confident. After all, such religious magnanimity hadn't been extended to the hostages during any other Muslim or Iranian holiday over the course of their nearly nine months of captivity. Why would this Ramadan be different? Considering the daily executions carried out by the regime against anti-Khomeini "coup plotters"—and purges against government and military officials considered not Islamic enough—it would appear that fasting and praying were not arousing any particular compassion towards the hostages.

It is perhaps for this reason that the official statement on the Shah's demise released by the Carter administration made no direct mention of the embassy staff. And, as if this weren't appalling enough, the announcement concluded with was a pathetic plea to the Iranian regime. "His death marks the end of an era in Iran, which all hope will be followed by peace and stability."[90]

Interestingly, Iranians didn't treat the news as the "end of an era." In fact, the Shah's passing didn't make as grand a set of headlines in his country as might have been expected by Americans—especially those who believed that if the US had only returned the former autocrat to his country, the whole crisis would have been shorter, if not averted altogether.

According to Laingen, who was witnessing growing fears among the Foreign Ministry staff that they were in genuine danger (now that their boss, Ghotzbzadeh, was a target of the Islamists and soon-to-be out of a job), the biggest "scoop" in the local papers was that the CIA had killed the Shah.

Far more attention was paid to the event in Cairo. On July 30, Egyptian President Sadat held a state funeral for the leader he had taken in when nobody else wanted him. Pahlevi was buried in the royal Al-Rafa'i Mosque. The only representative from the United States in attendance was former President Richard Nixon.

Ironically or not, this event coincided with an ABC/Harris poll showing that Carter's approval rating was even lower than Nixon's was during the Watergate scandal.

Meanwhile, as pro-Shah demonstrations were taking place in London, clashes between Khomeini loyalists and opponents, all Iranian nationals, were going on in Washington. The latter were exploited by Khomeini, who accused American police of brutality towards "peaceful" demonstrators. He then compared their actions to his own "humane" treatment of the US "spies" being held in Iran. He pointed to Richard Queen, whose illness was of such concern to him that he removed the young man's shackles of captivity.

The next day, Carter "told Ed [Muskie], over some reluctance on his part, to go ahead and send a message to our European allies urging them to work on the hostage release now that the Majlis had chosen a Speaker [Ali Akbar Hashemi Rafsanjani], the prime minister [Mohammed Ali Rajai] had been nominated, and the Shah's funeral was over."[91]

Though he said of this exchange that "the State Department moves like cold molasses," Carter was having what he described as "a very good day."[92] This may have been a function of the time he was devoting to drafts of the acceptance speech he was hopeful about giving at the Democratic National Convention in two weeks' time.

CHAPTER SEVEN

August 1980-January 1981

On August 14, a jubilant Carter stood at a podium in New York City's Madison Square Garden to accept his party's nomination as the candidate to run against Ronald Reagan in the November presidential election.

He now had the chance to deliver the speech that he had been working on for weeks. In the long and impassioned address, he made only one small reference to the embassy staff.

"My thoughts and prayers for our hostages in Iran are as though they were my own sons and daughters," he assured the crowd, after explaining that what he had learned on the job so far was that the presidency "is a place of compassion."

The gist of his statements to his fellow democrats was that they were both morally superior and far more realistic than their Republican counterparts, who lived in "a make-believe world, a world of good guys and bad guys..."

"Some have said it makes no difference who wins the election," he said. "They are wrong. This election is a stark choice between ... two futures. The year 2000 is just less than 20 years away... Children born this year will come of age in the 21st century. The time to shape the world of the year 2000 is now. The decisions of the next few years will set our course, perhaps an irreversible course..."

As for his vision: "I see a future of peace ... born of wisdom and based on a fairness toward all countries of the world... And I see risk ... of international confrontation, the risk of an uncontrollable, unaffordable, and unwinnable nuclear arms race..."

Accusing the Republicans of being "irresponsible" for wanting to achieve nuclear superiority, he explained why his path was far more pragmatic.

"It's simple to call for a new arms race," he said. "But when armed aggression threatens world peace, tough-sounding talk like that is not enough. A President must act responsibly. When Soviet troops invaded Afghanistan, we moved quickly to take action. I suspended some grain sales to the Soviet Union; I called for draft registration; and I joined wholeheartedly with the Congress and with the Olympic Committee and led more than 60 other nations in boycotting the big propaganda show in Russia—the Moscow Olympics..."

In his concluding remarks, Carter indicated he was proud of his accomplishments thus far.

"As I look back at my first term, I'm grateful that we've had a country for the full 4 years of peace," he asserted. "And that's what we're going to have for the next 4 years—peace... We've been tested under fire. We've neither ducked nor hidden, and we've tackled the great central issues of our time..."

Finally, he warned that the country would be in a sorry state of affairs in the event of his electoral defeat.

"If we succumb to a dream world, then we'll wake up to a nightmare," he said.[93]

The hostages couldn't have said it better themselves.

Oh, Brother

The overwhelming summer swelter was nothing compared to the heat on Carter during the first two weeks of August. Though a source of great anticipation and anxiety, the Democratic National Convention was the lesser of the hurdles the president had to overcome that month.

The first was the August 4 opening session of a special Senate subcommittee hearing on Carter's brother's dubious financial dealings with Libya. The affair—which came to be referred to as "Billygate"—had begun well before the embassy takeover in Iran. As part of a ploy to get around official trade bans imposed on the Qaddafi regime, the Libyan government had begun cultivating connections with individual businessmen in America. This they did by treating them to lavish trips to Tripoli, and securing return invitations to the US.

Billy Carter, who had a failed beer business under his belt and was now running a gas station, couldn't have been a better target. Not only was he an alcoholic with money woes, a big mouth and a visible chip on his shoulder; he was the brother of the US president. Appealing to his pocket and ego for the purpose of securing arms and oil deals would be a piece of cake—which it was.

As hostile media reports of Billy's hosting of a Libyan delegation began to emerge, along with anti-Semitic remarks he had made, the administration attempted to dissociate itself from the president's younger sibling. It might even have been somewhat successful at doing so.

But then came the November 4 embassy siege in Tehran. As the days passed, and it became apparent that it wasn't going to be resolved as quickly as Carter had hoped, the First Lady decided to take matters into her own hands. On November 19, at the beginning of the third week of the hostage crisis, Rosalynn Carter phoned her brother-in-law to ask whether he thought his Libyan friends might be able to help secure the release of the hostages. He said he thought they could.

When Rosalynn told her husband about the exchange, Carter contacted Brzezinski and asked him to follow up directly with Billy, which he did. Billy said he'd be glad to help, but he wanted permission from Secretary of State Vance before getting "involved between two governments."

When Brzezinski discussed this with Vance, he said it "might well be worth a try." Vance then phoned Billy and told him his department would not object to his trying to get the Libyans to urge Iran to release the hostages.

On November 22—three days after Rosalynn's phone call to Billy—the Libyan Foreign Secretariat issued a public statement about its desire for the hostages' release. This turned out to have had nothing to do with Billy Carter's key Libyan connection, Ali el-Houderi. In fact, neither he nor any administration officials had been able to reach Houderi by phone for days.

Still, that the administration not only knew of Billy Carter's dealings with Libya, but ultimately tried to utilize them, didn't look good for the president.

On the evening after the Senate subcommittee hearings on "Billygate" began, Carter gave a press conference. As was the case with his acceptance speech, he had been working hard on completing a report to Congress and on the statements he was going to make to the media about his brother.

That night, he was pleased as punch with himself for his performance—and hoped that "this entire process [would] help reestablish

Billy in the public mind as a reasonably responsible person..."[94]

Once he'd survived that, and emerged as the victor at the convention, Carter was now free to focus on eliminating what he considered the biggest threat to himself and his country—Ronald Reagan.

"My main problem," he assessed, "is still the opinion of the American people that I am not a strong leader and have inadequate vision for the future."[95]

Meanwhile, in Iran, Bani-Sadr was having his own "popularity" concerns, though not with any voting public. There it was with the ruling mullahs dismissing any of his decisions or choices for ministerial posts.

Fall Flurries

The day the administration in Washington had been waiting for was the source of renewed speculation and anticipation. It was September 10 when the Majlis finally approved a cabinet. Hoping Khomeini was a man of his word, Carter wanted to believe the ayatollah's assurances that the hostage crisis would be dealt with as soon as there was an official government in Tehran, with all ministers in place.

The next day, on September 11, Carter told Brzezinski to prepare a list of everything the US had been willing to offer in exchange for the hostages. He had learned that the day before, members of Khomeini's inner circle had given a message to German Ambassador to Iran Gerhard Ritzel. This was that the hostages would be released on three conditions: that all Iranian assets be unfrozen and transferred out of the US; that the commit to political and military non-intervention in Iranian affairs; and that the Shah's assets be returned to Iran.

According to Gary Sick, because this was the first communication from Khomeini since the taking of the hostages ten months earlier—and since previous dealings had turned out to be false—there was apprehension in the White House that this, too, might be a dead end.

Still, it was a straw at which to grasp—more than the administration had had since the botched rescue operation. Carter decided to grasp it when a radio speech delivered in Khomeini's name on September 12 concluded with the three conditions that had been conveyed through the German ambassador. Though a fourth condition was added—that the US would cancel any claims against Iran—it appeared that the start of a dialogue with Washington, this time, had backing and authority.

"This was the first time we were certain we were in direct contact with the ayatollah," Carter would later describe his relief. "And his position was both clear and rational."[96]

Indeed, Carter would have been only too happy to meet the ayatollah's demands, had there not been some technical/legal problems with the release of the Shah's assets. He made sure to let Khomeini know how pleased he was to get the ball rolling, in spite of the minor issues to be negotiated. This he did through Warren Christopher, his point-man for the secret meetings in Bonn, Germany with Khomeini's representative (and relative by marriage), Sadegh Tabatabai, a newly appointed cabinet minister.

Carter described Christopher's contacts with Tabatabai as "satisfactory." One thing the two sides seemed to have in common was the desire to resolve the hostage crisis before Americans went to the polls on November 4—a year to the date of the embassy siege. The American incumbent knew his chances for reelection would be well nigh dashed if the hostages were still in captivity by then. Nor were the Iranians too keen on having the likes of Reagan to confront in such a scenario. They, too, had heard the jokes about the Republican nominee that were beginning to surface. One riddle asked, "What's flat as a pancake and glows in the dark?" Its answer: "Iran, after Reagan becomes president."[97]

But, as should have been expected in Washington, every time progress appeared to be made on the ransom-for-the-hostages front, Tehran upped the ante. In spite of Carter's best efforts to appease his aggressors, they continued to create diversions and delays. If they were in a hurry to get the mess over with prior to the year anniversary, they had a funny way of going about it. Indeed, it would take a full two and a half months of negotiations after the presidential election (and through yet another intermediary, Algeria) before the hostages were released—on the day of Ronald Reagan's inauguration.

Iraq in the Mix

On September 22, Iraq invaded Iran. The age-old border disputes between the two countries—and the more recent emboldening of Iraqi Shi'ites siding with the Iranian Revolution—caused Iraq to launch a full-scale war.

Aiming to become the dominating force in the Persian Gulf, Iraq's Saddam Hussein decided to take advantage of the revolutionary unrest and factional disputes in Iran to attack from the air and on the ground.[98]

Laingen described the reaction he witnessed on the Iranian street as a result of the invasion. "...The mood in Tehran at the outset is one of confidence, excitement, patriotic and Islamic fervor, and rallying 'round the regime...buoyed by the traditional sense of Persian cultural and indeed racial superiority over the Arabs and particularly those from neighboring Iraq, with a people that had assaulted and converted to Islam the kingdoms of the high Persian plateaus in the eighth century."[99]

Laingen, like his bosses in Washington, was wondering how this new reality would affect the negotiations for the hostages. Unlike these bosses, however, Laingen and the rest of the embassy staff were hearing the air-raid sirens and explosions first-hand. Carter's greatest danger was of not being reelected; the hostages in Iran, on the other hand, were in palpable physical peril.

Still, the ability to move forward with negotiations was the key to their release at this point. And the first of several bad signs in this regard was the fact that the war broke out on the very day that Tabatabai was scheduled to return to Iran from Bonn, bearing tidings to Khomeini from Carter, via Warren Christopher. Because Tehran's airport had been bombed by Iraqi forces, Tabatabai's trip was cancelled. But even if he had been able to fly that day, it is unlikely that things would have progressed more quickly. This is because the message he was delivering was that the US couldn't guarantee waiving any and all future claims against Iran from the hostages; Christopher was going to have to go back home and receive further instructions.

As it turned out, of course, such "setbacks" prevented a deal from being struck before the November election and one-year anniversary of the embassy takeover.

A Gun to the Head

The tragic irony here is that Carter would eventually agree to waive any future claims against Iran. This was a move that would have consequences for decades. Indeed, for many years after their ordeal, the hostages tried to contest this waiver through legal channels, but to no avail.

Under the terms of the Algiers Accords—the agreement between the US and Iran that finally led to the release of the hostages[100]—no claims against Tehran from the hostages could be pursued at any time. No subsequent administration or Supreme Court has agreed to violate this or any other term of the accord, on the grounds that they constituted a legally binding and enduring US commitment to Iran.

Not even Congressional efforts, such as anti-state-sponsored terror-ism legislation, have changed the position of the courts on this matter.

This has not stopped the forty of the remaining living hostages—together with another hundred, or so, family members—from trying. They have always believed that the Algiers Accords constituted an ill-gotten ransom for their release. As it was coerced, they said, rather than agreed-upon in the conventional sense, it should not be "binding" or "enduring."

Prominent among these former hostages is Barry Rosen, who was serving as the embassy's press attaché when it was besieged. Today he heads the public and external affairs department at the Borough of Man-hattan Community College in New York City. In an interview with him in early 2011, while the case was heading to the appellate court, Rosen told me that the real impetus behind the lawsuit was no longer money ($6.6 billion). Rather, it has been the desire to make a harsh statement against Iran. The right to do this is something he feels he was robbed of—along with the 444 days of his life he can never recoup.

"Our main problem is with the State Department and the Justice Department," he explained. "Every time we have a case against Iran, they come in and discard it. So we really haven't gotten anywhere. Nor does it look like we'll win. It's been 30 years, and if it's 30 years, it can be never, too."

He is irked by the fact that "the United States has apologized to Iran about Mossadeq, but Iran has never apologized for what it did to us. And when the US shot down the Iranian air bus in the late '80s, it paid compensation to Iran for having made that terrible mistake."

So, as Rosen still harbors resentment against his captors, and against the culture which he says is one that suffers from "a lack of introspec-tion and with it the belief that everybody else is at fault for anything that befalls it," he is also angry that the signing of the Algiers Accords on the part of the Executive Branch is preventing him from seeking some kind of closure, if not justice.

Another Christmas in Captivity

During the two months of negotiations between the US and Iran, mediated by the Algerians, Carter's team had cause for repeated bouts of optimism followed by the fear of impasses created by Tehran. It is thus, then, that any anticipation that the hostages would be released by Christmas was quashed.

The hostages themselves couldn't believe that they were spending yet another family holiday away from home. And this time, unlike the last, the only clergy allowed in to see them were Iranian. In addition, the only "caroling" they were treated to, during the imposed power outages due to Iraqi air strikes, were air raid sirens.

Other visitors they received were members of an Algerian delegation, there to report back on the condition of the hostages, and reporters to conduct interviews showing "how well" the hostages were faring.

Back in America, where the National Christmas tree was lit for 417 seconds—one for each day of the hostages' captivity—the mood was one of anger at the helplessness of the government in getting the Iranians to accept a deal. There was also growing talk of what Reagan would do once in office, with speculation that he would go after Iran militarily.

Unlike the two colleagues held with him at the Foreign Ministry, Laingen was encouraged by the harshness of statements emanating from America. On December 27, he wrote:

"Indeed it is my view, with January 20 coming down the pike, that tough talk from Washington (particularly from Reagan himself) right now is *helpful* rather than harmful... There is some evidence, as a matter of fact, in a statement yesterday by the Iranian minister handling the talks via the Algerians, that the tactic may be working... As for the critical statements from the hostages' families, those in my view also keep the Iranians where they belong—on the defensive."[101]

The next day, Laingen was equally reassured. "Today's press (Voice Of America) quotes President-elect Reagan as responding to a question to the following effect: No we should not and cannot pay ransom to 'barbarians' who are guilty of 'kidnapping' diplomats. Bravo! That kind of background music from the man the Iranians will have to deal with after January 20 is welcome. Yes, there is a risk of an irrational response by the local fundamentalists, but that—in my view—is a risk worth taking in circumstances when Iran's need for a settlement is now painfully obvious to even the Iranian in the street."[102]

What he did not mention was the most urgent reason behind the Iranian government's need for a resolution to the crisis—Iraq. Reaching an agreement with the US would mean receiving all the American military equipment that had been withheld during the past year, which Iran desperately needed to continue fighting the war with its enemy neighbor.[103]

New Beginnings

On January 20, 1981, Ronald Reagan was sworn in as the fortieth president of the United States by Chief Justice Warren Burger. The ceremony constituted two historic firsts. It was the first time that the inauguration was held on the terrace of the Capitol building. And it was the first time that a new administration was taking the reins at the same moment that a national tragedy was coming to an abrupt end after 444 days.

Indeed, as Reagan got up to the podium to address the country whose leader he had now become, the 52 Americans who had spent a year and three months in Iranian captivity were boarding a plane out of Tehran.

In his speech, Reagan made no specific references to them. He did give an indirect message to Iran and the rest of the world about American will and power.

"…I believe we, the Americans of today, are ready to act worthy of ourselves, ready to do what must be done to ensure happiness and liberty for ourselves, our children and our children's children.

"And as we renew ourselves here in our own land, we will be seen as having greater strength throughout the world. We will again be the exemplar of freedom and a beacon of hope for those who do not now have freedom.

"To those neighbors and allies who share our freedom, we will strengthen our historic ties and assure them of our support and firm commitment. We will match loyalty with loyalty. We will strive for mutually beneficial relations. We will not use our friendship to impose on their sovereignty, for our own sovereignty is not for sale.

"As for the enemies of freedom, those who are potential adversaries, they will be reminded that peace is the highest aspiration of the American people. We will negotiate for it, sacrifice for it; we will not surrender for it—now or ever.

"Our forbearance should never be misunderstood. Our reluctance for conflict should not be misjudged as a failure of will. When action is required to preserve our national security, we will act. We will maintain sufficient strength to prevail if need be, knowing that if we do so we have the best chance of never having to use that strength.

"Above all, we must realize that no arsenal, or no weapon in the arsenals of the world, is so formidable as the will and moral courage of free men and women. It is a weapon our adversaries in today's world do not

have. It is a weapon that we as Americans do have. Let that be understood by those who practice terrorism and prey upon their neighbors."[104]

Outgoing President Carter was among those in attendance at the
inauguration. As he listened to the address, he was distracted by a nag-
ging worry that, in spite of the Algiers Accords, something would go
wrong and the hostages wouldn't be released.

His fears were put to rest, as he was informed by a Secret Service
agent at the ceremony that the hostages were on their way to Turkey.
This would be their first stop. Their second was Algeria. Their final destination before returning to the US was Germany, where they received
medical examinations.

The next day, Carter flew to meet them in Germany with some
trepidation. He was told that they were in far worse shape than had been
reported, and that many of them were angry at him for his handling of
their incarceration.

Nevertheless, Carter was greeted by them warmly, which both surprised and relieved him. After speaking to and answering questions from
the group, the now former president had photographs taken with each
hostage individually. The now-former First Lady watched the proceedings on the TV her husband had bought her for Christmas.

Carter returned home to Plains, Georgia the following day, to begin
the next chapter of his life—one of the most vociferously and actively
radical post-presidencies America has known.

Conspiracy Theories: a Post-Script to the Crisis

In the period leading up to Reagan's election, there was much speculation about whether Carter was planning an "October surprise"—a
last-minute maneuver to tip the scales in his favor at the ballot box in

November. This was largely due to a *Washington Post* news item about a piece it had refused to publish. The piece, which had been written by one of the paper's regular columnists, Jack Anderson, asserted that the president was amassing troops in the Persian Gulf, to pull off a massive invasion of Iran—just in time for the US election.[105]

Reaching the conclusion that Anderson's claim could not be corroborated—and quoting a sharp White House denial that any invasion was in the works—the *Post* canned the column. In so doing, rumors to the effect that Anderson's accusations must have been true ran rampant. Proof of how ridiculous they were became evident when no invasion—or any other military measure—took place.

What did occur, of course, was the incessant negotiating with Iran to give it what it wanted—which resulted in the release of the hostages, minutes after President Reagan's inauguration.

This fact, too, led to much speculation and rumor. The timing of the freeing of the abducted diplomats seemed suspicious. Had Reagan made a deal with the Iranians according to which they would hold off on the release of the hostages until he was safely in office? And if so, what did he have to offer in exchange?

More than a decade later, both Gary Sick and Bani-Sadr separately alleged that such an arrangement had been made. Sick even devoted an entire book to the subject.[106] However, after years of Congressional inquiries into the charges, it was concluded that they were false.

The Aftermath: From the Ayatollahs to the Arab Uprisings

There have been five presidents in the White House since then, counting Reagan: George H.W. Bush, Bill Clinton, George W. Bush and, currently, Obama. Each faced the consequences of Carter's policies.

Reagan ended détente with the Soviet Union, which he referred to as the "Evil Empire." He invaded Grenada—the first US military operation since the Vietnam War. He provided aid to militias in Central America and Afghanistan trying to overthrow their socialist governments.

Bush senior went to war against Saddam Hussein in Iraq, after he invaded Kuwait. The military offensive was halted after a mere 100 hours, however, leaving Saddam in power.

Under Clinton (who escaped an assassination attempt by terrorists in the Philippines who, it would emerge, were working for Osama bin Laden), the Battle of Mogadishu, during which many American soldiers were killed and wounded, resulted in the withdrawal of forces from Somalia.

During his presidency, NATO attacked Serbs in Bosnia, and he deployed US peacekeepers to uphold the Dayton Agreement.

Clinton also attacked terrorist targets in Afghanistan and Sudan, after a series of al-Qaeda bombings of US embassies in East Africa resulted in a dozen American deaths.

He would later authorize the use of US troops to assist in a NATO attack against Serbians in Kosovo.

Then Bush junior, confronted with the 9/11 attacks, invaded Afghanistan and Iraq. Many other related conflicts took place in the world. Among these were two Palestinian "intifadas" against Israeli civilians, and Hizbullah and Hamas missiles from Lebanon and Gaza, resulting in two Israeli wars against Islamic terrorism in those areas.

Ironically, the more the US and other Western countries came to acknowledge and try to overcome the threat posed by the long arm of Islamic fundamentalism and its inexorable link to terrorism, the more the aggressive phenomenon has grown. Embedding itself into the societies of countries across the globe through funding by Iran and Saudi Arabia, it has managed to mushroom, rather than be contained.

When he took office, President Obama believed that his "hope and change" agenda would be the solution if not the cure. It was his conviction that American and Israeli actions were largely responsible for the radicalization of the Arab and Muslim world. He would change all that by "reaching out" to those countries and groups which were threatening the security of innocent people around the globe. He would show them all he understood their gripes.

The eruption of the "Arab Spring" he has been championing—and taking much credit for—filled him with much self-satisfaction. Its outcome, however, is proving to be more like that of the Iranian Revolution than the American one.

As each autocrat is being toppled by angry mobs across the Middle East, it is becoming clear that what is replacing them is not democracy, but rather Islamic rule.

The events are still unfolding, with each country having a different set of circumstances. A good way to examine then as a whole is to look at Egypt.

PART II
THE FALL OF EGYPT

CHAPTER ONE

The Unraveling of
the Camp David Accords

"Allahu akbar! Allahu akbar!" the crowd at Cairo's Tahrir Square chanted hysterically. It was February 11, 2011, the day on which it was announced that Egyptian President Hosni Mubarak had finally succumbed to his ouster by the people he had ruled for nearly 30 years.[107] And he had fled to Sharm el-Sheikh, the Red Sea resort town that Egypt had gained as a result of its peace treaty with Israel three decades earlier.

"God is great!" they screamed at the tops of their lungs to express their joy at having been successful in their endeavor. For 18 days straight, they had been demonstrating for "freedom from tyranny and corruption."

Buoyed by the events in Tunisia, the Egyptian masses, too, had taken to the streets, demanding "death to the dictator."

As had been the case following the riots that led to the downfall of Tunisian President Ben Ali, both the Western media and the White

House observed the events in Egypt with optimism. The "Arab Spring" seemed to be bursting out all over the Middle East, thanks to President Barack Obama's olive-branch policies. Even many conservatives were pleased. The process of democratization that former President George W. Bush had strived for and set in motion was now on the verge of fruition.

The yearning for a better life in the Arab-Muslim world seemed to be spreading like a contagious virus, assisted by social networking on the Internet. Indeed, to the nostalgic anti-Vietnam War generation and its offspring, this so-called "Facebook Revolution" was a source of inspiration.

It was only fitting, then, that CBS should want to give special coverage to the phenomenon. To this end, Lara Logan, a correspondent for the network's hit show, "Sixty Minutes," was dispatched to Egypt to prepare an in-depth news feature.

But things didn't go so smoothly for Logan and her crew. A few days after arriving, they were arrested by the Egyptian military. Their driver was beaten, and they were handcuffed, blindfolded, detained over night and told to get out of the country.[108]

A week later, they were back, however, this time to cover the celebrations surrounding Mubarak's exit.

Logan couldn't have been more excited when she and the crew "drove from the airport into Cairo that night... it was unbelievable. It was like unleashing a champagne cork on Egypt."

Logan was "anxious to get to the square...because this is a moment in history that you don't want to miss." It looked like "a party," Logan later described. "...a roar of sound because everyone is so excited and they are singing songs of the revolution and shouting slogans."

Logan, a veteran journalist originally from South Africa, was not daunted. On the contrary, she had been in many difficult situations during her career—including in Egypt itself the week before, when she had been detained. And this event, if anything, was more joyous than dangerous.

Or so she thought.

For an entire hour, she and her crew managed to move through the throngs with no mishap, other than being jostled like everybody else in the packed square. But then the crew noticed that their camera battery was beginning to die, and they stopped for a moment to decide what to do about it.

It was during that pause that Logan was spotted by a group of men in the crowd. Immediately, their attention shifted from elation at having toppled Mubarak to Logan. The beautiful blonde in Western dress suddenly became the focus of a very different kind of glee.

"Let's take off her pants," one of them called out to the others. Logan did not understand the Arabic words, but her Egyptian fixer did. "We've got to get you out of here," he insisted. But it was too late. Dozens of male hands had begun swarming around her, groping her breasts and crotch.

"Stop!" she screamed, to no avail.

"You Jew!" one yelled. (Logan is not Jewish.)

"She's Israeli!" another chimed in. (Logan is certainly not Israeli.)

This served to fuel the already escalating molestation she had begun to endure. As a result of her being grabbed and pawed, her clothes were ripped from her body, and she was separated from the members of her crew. Suddenly, the tough correspondent was now a terrified victim of mass sexual abuse. All she could think about while being raped with hands and other objects, among them flagpoles, was staying alive for her two young children.

For twenty-five minutes straight, she was tugged at in all directions. Her battered, bruised, near-naked body was passed around among the approximately two hundred men participating in the ecstatic assault.

Logan thought that if she screamed, either they would stop or someone else would stop them, but "it was the opposite." The more she shouted for mercy, the more frenzied they became.

It is not likely Logan would have made it out of there alive had the gang who was raping her not run into a fence. Alongside the barrier, there was a group of chador-clad women, who had camped out for the demonstration-turned-celebration. It was they who took pity on Logan, fending off the men and encircling her long enough for some soldiers to arrive and beat off the aggressors with their batons.

Logan was flown back to the US immediately after her rescue. She was treated for internal injuries and severe muscle damage. When she recuperated, she gave interviews describing her ordeal, culminating in a tell-all with "Sixty Minutes."

The reason she provided for wanting to reveal the details of her assault, she explained, was to "add her voice to those who confront sexual violence; to break the code of silence."[109]

She told *The New York Times* that she wanted to "speak out about sexual violence both on behalf of other journalists and on behalf of 'millions of voiceless women who are subjected to attacks like this and worse.'"[110]

Where the former is concerned, Logan said that it is in "the very nature of what we do" that is "undoing these regimes. It makes us the enemy, whether we like it or not."[111] This is why she made a decision not to continue to cover the Middle East protests in the meantime.

Given the degree of her trauma, this is more than understandable. Less so is her attributing the hatred she experienced to her being "the enemy" by virtue of her profession—one that leads to the "undoing" of bad regimes. In fact, it was not the Mubarak regime or its supporters who were responsible for her rape. On the contrary, the men who mauled her were the "Facebook revolutionaries" who *favored* toppling the regime. The people who, she said, "really enjoyed my pain and suffering,"[112] were the very ones she and her colleagues had reported as engaged in a "non-violent" uprising spawned by the universal aspiration for better, freer lives.

Logan did admit that before her horrible experience in Cairo, she had not been aware of the extent to which women in Egypt and other Middle Eastern countries were suffering from abuse. "I would have paid more attention to it if I had had any sense of it. When women are harassed and subjected to this in society, they're denied an equal place in that society. Public spaces don't belong to them. Men control it [sic]. It reaffirms the oppressive role of men in the society."[113]

Logan's idea, like that of all "Arab Spring" optimists, is that the subjugation of women is one among many symptoms of oppressive, autocratic regimes. According to this logic, once those regimes are replaced, the People—among them women—can get down to the business of building more egalitarian societies for themselves. This was the kind of thinking that led American liberals to support the toppling of the Shah of Iran. It is the kind of thinking that caused President Obama, like Jimmy Carter before him, to hesitate about helping a long-time ally—and then to abandon him by siding with his adversaries. Women are a prime group who never have, and never will, benefit from such thinking and policies. Indeed, the next time Logan returns to Cairo—if she is ever emotionally up to it—she will undoubtedly be forced to do so, draped from head to toe in Islamic garb.[114] This is because, while the so-called freedom-loving youth was celebrating their new-found liberation, the previously banned Muslim Brotherhood and its more extreme brethren, the Salafists, were diligently organizing to take over.

They had good reason to believe they would succeed. Not only was Mubarak out of the way—which was cause enough for their certainty; but they had been given what they took to be a green light from no other than the president of the United States himself mere months after his inauguration.

Indeed it was Barack Obama who set the stage for what is emerging across the Middle East not as an "Arab Spring," but as an Islamist tidal wave.

Chapter Two

Bowing Down to His Brethren

In June, 2009, the recently instated "hope-and-change" leader of the Free World made it his first priority to engage in outreach to the Muslim world. His own upbringing in Indonesia—where he said he fondly remembered the chants of the imams emanating from minarets—was one reason for his empathy towards, if not affinity for, Islam. Another was his twenty-year affiliation with a church whose blatantly anti-Semitic pastor—the Rev. Jeremiah Wright—reinforced his sentiments.

It was Obama's conviction that America was partially responsible, if not outright to blame, for its bad reputation around the globe, particularly among Third World Muslims. It was not clear whether he understood the events of 9/11 in this context. But he certainly viewed its aftermath—the outbreak of what he and others called "Islamophobia"—to be a disease that needed eradication. And he was going to be the president to provide the antidote.

To this end, he set about to persuade any and all of his country's adversaries that he was, in fact, their friend. Among his first orders of business as president was to make a pilgrimage to the Middle East. His first stop was Saudi Arabia, where he bowed down to the king. His second was Egypt, where he bowed down to the entire Muslim-Arab world from the podium of the University of Cairo. Indeed, on June 4, the president of the United States spelled out his foreign policy in front of thousands of Egyptians. One key figure was glaringly absent in the packed hall, however. Due to the abundance of Muslim Brotherhood members and supporters in the auditorium, Egyptian President Hosni Mubarak refused to attend.

This did not prevent Obama from doing what he had set out to do—which was to embrace Muslims of all stripes. He was determined not to make petty distinctions between radicals and non-radicals, between Sunnis and Shiites, between terrorists and anti-terrorists, between groups allied with Iran or those attempting to be extricated from Iran's proxies. No, Obama was not going to make the "mistake" of his nemesis, George W. Bush—or his more distant predecessor, Ronald Reagan—by calling on the world to choose between good and evil. Obama was going to be a more Carter-like diplomat, showing the rest of the world that he understood their gripes against America, and that he would listen and learn from them.

"*Assalaamu alaykum* [peace be with you]," he said, extending an Arabic greeting *only* used when one Muslim is addressing another (which the audience necessarily perceived as Obama's way of saying he himself was one of them). "We meet at a time of tension between the United States and Muslims around the world... fed by colonialism that denied rights and opportunities to many Muslims, and a Cold War in which Muslim-majority countries were too often treated as proxies without regard to their own aspirations. Moreover, the sweeping change brought by modernity and globalization led many Muslims to view the West as hostile to the traditions of Islam.

"Violent extremists have exploited these tensions in a small but potent minority of Muslims. The attacks of September 11, 2001 and the continued efforts of these extremists to engage in violence against civilians has led some in my country to view Islam as inevitably hostile not only to America and Western countries, but also to human rights... "

Due to his chief concern that the West shouldn't make sweeping, prejudicial judgments due to 9/11, Obama asserted that he had "come here to seek a new beginning between the United States and Muslims around the world." And then he made the first of many references to the "Holy Koran," from which he quoted: "Be conscious of God and speak always the truth." This, said the US president, "is what I will try to do..."

To show that he was not merely an American Christian, but rather someone who understood the Muslim mindset and was heartened by it, he recounted, "...As a boy, I spent several years in Indonesia and heard the call of the azaan at the break of dawn and the fall of dusk. As a young man, I worked in Chicago communities where many found dignity and peace in their Muslim faith. As a student of history, I also know civilization's debt to Islam..."

After waxing poetic about Islam's having been responsible for much of the world's mathematical, architectural and other innovations of cultural and scientific significance, he went on to laud its humanitarianism.

"...Islam has demonstrated through words and deeds the possibilities of religious tolerance and racial equality," he said, adding that it "has always been a part of America's story... Since our founding, American Muslims have enriched the United States. And I consider it part of my responsibility as President of the United States to fight against negative stereotypes of Islam wherever they appear."

The stunned and exuberant Muslim Brotherhood-heavy audience couldn't believe their ears. To have such a champion in the Oval Office—one whose stated objective was to look out for *their* interests the world over—was more than they had bargained for when they prayed to Allah for him to be elected.

Nor did the rest of Obama's tribute and assurances disappoint.

"...Freedom in America is indivisible from the freedom to practice one's religion," he continued. "That is why there is a mosque in every state of our union, and over 1,200 mosques within our borders. That is why the US government has gone to court to protect the right of women and girls to wear the hijab, and to punish those who would deny it. So let there be no doubt: Islam is a part of America."

As for America's role regarding Islamic countries, he said: "...Human history has often been a record of nations and tribes subjugating one another to serve their own interests. Yet in this new age, such attitudes are self-defeating. Given our interdependence, any world order that elevates one nation or group of people over another will inevitably fail... America is not—and never will be—at war with Islam... Islam is not part of the problem in combating violent extremism—it is an important part of promoting peace."

Another issue he addressed was nuclear weapons—"a source of tension between the United States and the Islamic Republic of Iran."

"For many years," he said, "Iran has defined itself in part by its opposition to my country, and there is indeed a tumultuous history between us. In the middle of the Cold War, the United States played a role in the overthrow of a democratically-elected Iranian government. Since the Islamic Revolution, Iran has played a role in acts of hostage-taking and violence against US troops and civilians...

"Rather than remain trapped in the past, I have made it clear to Iran's leaders and people that my country is prepared to move forward...

"It will be hard to overcome decades of mistrust, but we will proceed with courage, rectitude and resolve. There will be many issues to discuss between our two countries, and we are willing to move forward without preconditions on the basis of mutual respect...

"No single nation should pick and choose which nations hold nuclear weapons. That is why I strongly reaffirmed America's commitment to seek a world in which no nations hold nuclear weapons. And any nation—including Iran—should have the right to access peaceful nuclear power if it complies with its responsibilities under the nuclear Non-Proliferation Treaty..."

As he made his point about no country having the right to "choose which nations hold nuclear weapons," so, too, did Obama make clear to the Muslim-Arab world that "no system of government can or should be imposed upon one nation by any other... America does not presume to know what is best for everyone..."

As for "religious freedom," he claimed that "Islam has a proud tradition of tolerance... [that] is essential for religion to thrive, but it is being challenged in many different ways.

"Among some Muslims, there is a disturbing tendency to measure one's own faith by the rejection of another's...

"Freedom of religion is central to the ability of peoples to live together. We must always examine the ways in which we protect it. For instance, in the United States, rules on charitable giving have made it harder for Muslims to fulfill their religious obligation. That is why I am committed to working with American Muslims to ensure that they can fulfill zakat.

"Likewise, it is important for Western countries to avoid impeding Muslim citizens from practicing religion as they see fit—for instance, by dictating what clothes a Muslim woman should wear. We cannot disguise hostility towards any religion behind the pretence of liberalism...

"That is why we welcome efforts like Saudi Arabian King Abdullah's Interfaith dialogue and Turkey's leadership in the Alliance of Civilizations. Around the world, we can turn dialogue into Interfaith service, so bridges between peoples lead to action..."

Then the president went on to talk about women's rights, which—he stressed—"are by no means simply an issue for Islam. In Turkey, Pakistan, Bangladesh, and Indonesia, we have seen Muslim-majority countries elect a woman to lead. Meanwhile, the struggle for women's equality continues in many aspects of American life."

Obama ended his speech to a crowd not exactly enthused by Western influence on its culture and political goals by pointing out the advantages of globalization.

"There need not be contradiction between development and tradition," he stated. "...In ancient times and in our times, Muslim communities have been at the forefront of innovation and education..."

He then asserted his intention to invest in and expand exchange programs for economic and other cooperative efforts between America and Muslim countries, including "a new global effort with the Organization of the Islamic Conference[115] to eradicate polio."

To sum up his lengthy appeal to—and appeasement of—the holders of the faith to which he attributed the same aspirations as those of his own countrymen, the new president of the United States concluded: "The people of the world can live together in peace. We know that is God's vision. Now, that must be our work here on Earth."

Cautiously Positive Reactions

Following Obama's "historic" speech in Cairo, every media outlet with bureaus in Muslim countries rushed to provide both man-in-the-street reactions and quotes from religious and political leaders. The consensus—if there, indeed, was such a thing—was that the president's words were "a good beginning, but needed to be backed up with actions." After years of American "colonialism" and "support for Israel due to the 'Zionist lobby' in Washington," it was not enough for the new leader to make pronouncements about his sympathy and intentions. He was going to have to prove himself to them.

One encouraging omen was that Obama did not make a stop next door in Israel during his trip to Egypt, but rather left for Europe after being given a tour of the Pyramids and Sphinx. It was an unusual move for an American leader to be in the Middle East without also paying a call on Jerusalem.

CHAPTER THREE

From Cairo to Jerusalem

One president who *had* made the very short journey, travel-wise (a mere hour by plane)—yet great distance in every other way—to see the Israeli prime minister was Anwar Sadat.

The year was 1977, the event unprecedented. It was the start of the 35-year treaty between Egypt and Israel for which Jimmy Carter took undeserved credit—and whose imminent demise can be justifiably attributed to Barack Obama. A good way to understand why the former was significant and the latter a disaster for the West is to review a bit of Egyptian history.

Dan Schueftan, Middle East scholar and director of the National Security Studies Center at the University of Haifa, says it all began in 1956. In an interview with him prior to the outbreak of the "Arab Spring," Schueftan said that this was the year when Egypt's second president, Gamal Abdel Nasser ("an insignificant leader of a poor, miserable country") ushered the Soviets into the Mediterranean. Through his arms deal with

Communist Czechoslovakia the year before, Nasser had "undermined the entire global strategy of the United States by enabling the USSR to position itself in the 'soft underbelly of Europe.'"

"Faced with this threat," he explained, "Britain and France wanted to take serious action. They wanted to do to Egypt what the US would do to Iraq in the 2000s—to break anybody threatening their interests and sending the message 'Don't fuck with us' to everybody else. Though Europe by this time was no longer a superpower, it still had the state of mind of one. The US was exactly the opposite: It had the power without the mentality.

"Indeed, President Eisenhower decided to suddenly speak on behalf of what we call today the 'international community.' And not only did he tell the Brits and the French to leave, but he humiliated them. This was on the American assumption that the Arabs and non-aligned states were accusing the US of being the new colonialists. And Eisenhower was concerned with proving that it wasn't so. He thought the way to do that was by breaking the colonialists to show Nasser and other Arab leaders that American intentions were good.

"But this is not the thinking of a major power. This is the thinking of a minor, insignificant state. A power doesn't need to be understood in terms of how 'nice' it is, but rather how powerful. What you want to instill in people is not love, but respect—especially in the Middle East.

"Nasser, meanwhile, understood that it was worth his while to be pro-Soviet and anti-American, because if you're pro-Soviet and anti-American, the Soviets support you, and because you're pro-Soviet and anti-American, the Americans also support you!

"And the whole Arab world cheered Nasser, who, as they saw it, defeated the British and the French, and humiliated the Americans. This is how Nasser became the ultimate leader, threatening all pro-Western regimes... and by 1957, any regime in the Middle East that was pro-American, pro-Western, or not radical collapsed or was on the brink of collapse."

John F. Kennedy, the president following Eisenhower, was "no great genius either" when it came to Middle East policy, said Schueftan. Fearing the further radicalization and anti-Americanism of the region, Kennedy believed that the way to get Egypt to appreciate the US was to provide food for its starving population. This was in spite of the fact that the reason Nasser had no money to feed his people was that he was spending it all on weapons' purchases from the USSR. "The idea that hungry Egyptians would become even more radical and anti-American than they already were, and therefore that the US had to feed them, was like committing suicide for fear of death," he said.

"And then came Lyndon Johnson, the guy who understood that radicals need to be broken. After the Six Day War in 1967, Nasser wanted to force the US to pursue what he himself called a '1957 policy.' This meant getting Israel to relinquish everything it had gained in the war in exchange for nothing—a move that would strengthen his position in the Arab world and satisfy the Soviets. He assumed that America would automatically go along with this. His idea was that all American presidents must be stupid, since they believed that bad guys can become good guys if they are treated nicely.

"But Johnson wasn't like his predecessors. What he did was to make American assistance to Egypt *conditional*. He said to Nasser: 'Yes, you may have your territory back, but you will have to move from a Soviet orientation to an American one.'

"Johnson's successor, Richard Nixon, continued with this policy. When push came to shove in the War of Attrition, Nixon supported putting pressure on Egypt, to force Egypt to realize that it could not make the US alter its policy in any way that would benefit the Soviet Union—

not even under threat of a confrontation between Egypt and Israel that could potentially cause a nuclear clash between the US and the USSR."

This required courage and ultimately paid off, according to Scheuftan.

In 1970, when Nasser died, Anwar Sadat became Egypt's third president. Though himself a Nasser loyalist, Sadat was seen by the officials left over from the previous regime as a weak, puppet-like figure who could be easily manipulated. He was intent on proving them wrong, and on clinging to his newfound power for dear life. To do so, he would have to be clever on three fronts: the Arab world, which was watching to see how he would compare to their hero, Nasser; the United States, which he understood he could not challenge without financial repercussions; and Israel, his country's arch enemy.

In 1973, Sadat launched a war against the neighboring Jewish state from its southern border, together with Syria's Hafez al-Assad, who attacked it from the north. The assault, which was joined by other surrounding Arab countries, came to be called the Yom Kippur War. It was staged purposely on the Jewish (high holy) Day of Atonement, when most Israelis were fasting and praying in synagogues, to provide the weaker armies the advantage of surprise.

As Schueftan explained, "Sadat realized that Israel was much stronger militarily than Egypt. This is why all he really wanted was a short war during which he could threaten Israel in a very limited way, for a very short period of time, on a very narrow stretch of land. His strategy was to launch the surprise attack, and then, after the Israelis overcame the surprise and regained the upper hand, he would capitulate to the United States under favorable conditions."

Indeed, as soon as Israel was about to deal Egypt a final crushing blow in the war, Sadat turned to Nixon's Secretary of State, Henry Kissinger, and proposed a deal that would involve Egypt's making a dramatic change in its orientation, from pro-Soviet to pro-American. The Nixon administration wanted to use this turn of events to create what Scheuftan called a "win-win-win situation."

According to this approach, what America would gain was having the most important country in the Third World shifting its allegiance to the United States. What Israel would gain—in exchange for not declaring a military victory—was the absence of war with its southernmost hostile neighbor for a very long time (since Egypt would now depend on US aid, and no country dependent on America at that time could wage war against Israel.)

What Egypt would gain was the perception in the Arab world that it had scored a huge victory over Israel, while getting everything it wanted from America as well as being free of confrontation with a formidable enemy it had not been able to beat.

"Sadat invested a huge amount of energy and political capital in trying to make this work," said Schueftan, "and it all hinged on the ability to pull off a trilateral agreement involving Egypt, Israel, and the United States—without the pull of the radical forces of Syria, the PLO, and the Soviet Union."

It is this that led to the 1974 "Israel-Egypt Separation of Forces Agreement," immediately following the war, and subsequently to the 1975 "Interim Agreement," according to which Israel would withdraw from territory in the Sinai as part of an eventual peace deal, and the "Israel-United States Memorandum of Understanding."

The balancing act was a delicate one for Sadat, made more complicated by the fact that, in the midst of it all, Nixon ended up resigning as a result of the Watergate scandal. Gerald Ford, who was catapulted, rather than voted, into the US presidency, was now going to have to pick up the ball.

But at least he, Kissinger, Sadat, and Israeli Prime Minister Yitzhak Rabin all knew that the key to any mutually beneficial arrangement was to keep the Soviet Union and its proxies out of the process.

Enter Jimmy Carter, Stage Left

When Ford was defeated in 1976 by his opponent from the Democratic Party—a relatively unknown governor from Georgia, previously a peanut farmer—it wasn't clear what direction American foreign policy would take. However, one thing about him appeared to be a given, due to his history and his campaign slogans: He was as anti-Communist as they come. Or so it seemed at the time.

The first thing Carter did when he took office was to assert that he was going to be a different kind of American president, one who showed the world that the United States was a "good guy," concerned mainly with human rights and non-proliferation of nuclear weapons.

Regarding the Middle East, his attitude was that there would have to be a comprehensive peace between Israel and its Arab neighbors. The slow "step-by-step" approach of his immediate predecessors would be a thing of the past. In other words, a mere bilateral arrangement between Israel and Egypt, backed by the US, would not suffice to bring about a multilateral Middle East reconciliation.

He would bring all the key parties to Geneva—including the Syrians, the PLO, *and* the Soviet Union. He would be the New Messiah.

Menachem Begin, who became Israel's prime minister a few months after Carter was inaugurated, was not the only leader who knew that this was a dangerous idea. Sadat, too, understood how disastrous it would be for his own strategy. He wanted to do things differently from Nasser, by making a deal with Israel and moving closer to the United States—yet gain a "victory" and territory in the process. Ironically, then, it was Begin and Sadat who wanted to make a deal—each for his own reasons—and it was Carter who threatened to sabotage the whole thing.

"Anybody who was not a complete idiot knew that the inevitable result of Carter's delusions of grandeur would be failure. There wasn't a chance in a zillion that his plan of a comprehensive peace would work. If you gave veto power to radicals, you'd be finished. And if you brought in the Soviet Union, which didn't want such a deal anyway, and the Syrians, who were committed to a completely different approach, and the Palestinians, who were inherently irresponsible, the chances of a settlement were zero, while the chances of confrontation were very high."

Sadat, therefore, had to see to it that there would be no Geneva conference. The way he did this was by making his historical trip to Jerusalem. Carter could hardly come out against this bold, "peace-seeking" public gesture, which was greeted by great fanfare in the West. He had no choice, then, but to embrace it, so as not to lose face. He also had to make sure that he did not appear to be running up from behind to catch up to the unfolding drama. Otherwise, he wouldn't have been able to take center stage and win the "Emmy" for best producer and director. Indeed, when all was said and done, under his "auspices," he would be awarded the Nobel Peace Prize along with Sadat and Begin. But, whereas Sadat would end up assassinated by Muslim Brotherhood and Salafist radicals for his treaty with Israel and alliance with the US, and Begin would become depressed and reclusive until his death, Carter has been happily using his Nobel laurels to this day to further his foolish and dangerous agenda.

The Rise of Mubarak

Sadat was assassinated on October 6, 1981, after leading Egypt for 11 years. When he took over, he made a move that would have serious consequences. As part of a "rectification revolution," he released Islamist activists who had been jailed during Nasser's rule. For a while, this— and his supposed victory over Israel in the Yom Kippur War—kept the radicals in his corner. As soon as he began negotiating with the United States and Israel, however, they wanted him and his regime stamped out. To this end, they began recruiting members of the military. They gathered weapons and manpower, and lay in wait for the right moment to kill the secular "traitor" and all the members of his top echelon, to raid all government institutions—including the TV and radio—and to announce the beginning of an Islamist revolution in Egypt. Though the plot was discovered, and members of the Egyptian Islamic Jihad cells were arrested, another key cell, the Islamic Group, evaded authorities. This cell was led by "Blind Sheikh" Omar Abdel-Rahman (who would subsequently mastermind the 1993 World Trade Center bombings). And it was the Blind Sheik's *fatwa* that led to the murder of Sadat, while he was watching the annual parade marking Egypt's victory in the Yom Kippur War. During the attack, eleven other attendees were killed and twenty-eight people wounded, among them Vice President Mubarak, who survived—with an injured hand—to replace the dead leader.

When Mubarak took over, the first thing he did was to beef up the country's security forces. This was not only due to his having had a long-standing military career, which caused him to have an affinity that his predecessors lacked. It was also because he had witnessed Sadat's assassination first-hand, as well as nearly getting killed himself, during the massacre at the parade in Cairo.

Indeed, one of the things that characterized Mubarak's reign, as opposed to that of Egypt's previous three presidents, was that he con-sulted with army officers and other security personnel, rather than with political advisors, on matters of state. And his chief internal concern was keeping the Muslim radicals under investigation, under suspicion and, above all, under control. It was as much in his interest to do so—if not more so—than that of the Israelis, with whom he upheld the Camp David Accords for the next three decades. To be sure, this produced a far colder peace than much of the Israeli public had fantasized it would be. While Israeli tourists flooded Cairo and other cities practically the second the treaty was a done deal, to take in the culture and spend a lot of hard-earned shekels to see belly dancers perform and to take photos of their families on camels by the Pyramids, the state-run Egyptian media continued to vilify Zionists and Jews. Needless to say, Egyptians did not flock to Jerusalem and Tel Aviv to take in the ambiance or the night life. This was only partly due to their wariness of their neighbors across the border. More likely it was because they were too busy trying to eke out the most meager of wages to put food on their tables. Nevertheless, it was understood that the Mubarak regime and the Israeli government (led every few years by someone else) shared a common patron—the United States—and a common threat, the Muslim Brotherhood. If anybody understood the repercussions of a secular regime falling into the hands of radical clerics it was Mubarak. After all, he had been privy to the close relationship that Sadat had had with the Shah of Iran—who was buried in Cairo following his ouster and exile by the Ayatollah Khomeini.

As in the case of the Shah, Mubarak had to maneuver a delicate balancing act between satisfying American insistence on his providing greater freedoms for his people and keeping a very tight leash on anyone who might pose a threat to his regime. This took the form, for example, of his allowing "free" elections for parliament, on the one hand, and outlawing any and all parties which posed such a threat, on the other. It was thus that the (Iranian-backed) Muslim Brotherhood had been banned from taking part in Egyptian politics for the last several decades.

Undemocratic though the system may have been, it has served the United States well—and not only as a result of Sadat's choice to switch sides in the Cold War.

When Iraq invaded Kuwait on August 2, 1990, Egypt was among the first countries to join the United States in condemning the move. It was also a key player in the UN-approved war waged by US President George H. W. Bush against Iraqi despot Saddam Hussein. Mubarak allowed the US to use Egyptian air space and the Suez Canal for the purpose of amassing American troops in Saudi Arabia. He then sent two divisions of his army to Kuwait, to participate in the fighting on the ground. This was not only technically crucial; it was ideologically so, as well. Due to Egypt's powerful status in the Arab world, Mubarak's efforts gave legitimacy to other Arab countries to jump on the coalition bandwagon. Mubarak was rewarded for this by having a huge chunk of his national debt forgiven—which is the stuff that mutual interests are made of, after all.

This alliance had its ups and downs during the subsequent presidencies of Bill Clinton and George W. Bush. It was good for America. It was good for Egypt—though cause for much rumbling on the part of Mubarak's oppositionists, who wanted him to join Sadat in the hell reserved for apostates. In fact, it is said that he escaped at least six assassination attempts during his time in power. The only country in the Camp David triumvirate for which it was less than ideal was Israel.

For one thing, Mubarak frequently appointed himself mediator between Israel and the Palestinians, as well as "peace-maker" between the Palestinian Authority and Hamas. Because of the Hamas charter requiring the destruction of the Jewish state, a reconciliation with the PA would not only have made a deal with Israel more impossible than it already was (since the PA itself never was a genuine negotiating partner to begin with), but it would serve to further radicalize the Palestinian-populated areas in Israel's midst.

In addition, when Israel withdrew from the Gaza Strip in 2005—forfeiting a key strategic security buffer—it did so with assurances from the United States that it would be protected, and from Mubarak that he would police the border Egypt shared with Gaza.

This did not stop the Muslim Brotherhood terrorists in Egypt from smuggling massive amounts of arms to their counterparts in Gaza, all of whom are financed by Iran. They did this by building primitive tunnels through which they transferred weapons on a daily basis. The Egyptian military, tasked with preventing such occurrences, was slacking off on the job. This was partly due to ineptitude, and partly because its chief concern always was keeping its palms greased by being in charge of bread production and distribution. Basically, the military in Egypt looked out for itself. And if it was successful in following Mubarak's orders to keep the Muslim Brotherhood at bay, this was because it did not have any interest in sharing its power with anyone.

The result of the tunneling of materiel into Gaza was incessant rocket-fire against civilians in southern Israel. The irony here is that the ostensible reason Prime Minister Ariel Sharon disengaged from Gaza in the first place was the increased infiltration from there of suicide bombers, who blew themselves up on buses and shopping malls in cities throughout Israel. Leaving the territory and fencing it off was his way of putting a stop to the carnage. Though the plan succeeded in hindering the movement of individual terrorists into Israel, it did nothing to stop the missile fire from Gaza into southern Israel. In fact, the launching of rockets that had been sporadic up to this point became more than a daily occurrence, forcing many Israelis to spend hours—and sometimes days—at a time in bomb shelters.

In 2006, the missiles started flying into Israel over its northern border, as well, when the Hizbullah in Lebanon joined in the festivities. Iran, whose president was threatening to "wipe Israel off the map," was using these proxies to help get the job done. (This led to the Second Lebanon War in 2006 and Operation Cast Lead at the end of 2008.)

As bad as this situation was for Israel, it would have been far worse had Mubarak not been hanging on to his alliance with the United States.

CHAPTER FOUR

Obama Undoes the Knot

As the beautiful and enthusiastic reporter, Lara Logan, was being torn limb-from-limb by cheerful freedom-seekers in the streets of Cairo, Barack Obama was safely home at the White House, helping his speech writers put the finishing touches on the statement he was about to make in response to Mubarak's resignation.

Since the US president had contributed to this turn of events, he was pleased, finally, to be able to be able to say something positive about the goings-on in Egypt. For the duration of the nearly three weeks of demonstrations that had been taking place at Tahrir Square, his administration had been sending harsh messages to Mubarak, warning him not to quell the rebellion, and threatening to cut off aid if he used force or other measures to do so.[116]

This was in spite of the fact that Mubarak was attempting to give in to the demands of the demonstrators and the White House. In fact, the Egyptian leader had made a televised address on February 1, during which he vowed to enact political reforms, to bow out of the presidential election slated for September, and to remove himself from office after overseeing a peaceful transition to the next government.

His pledge not only had been unsatisfactory to the people in the streets, but served to fan the flames of their rage even further. Obama followed their lead. The protests, he reiterated, were their right. And the time had come for the Egyptian president to join his Tunisian counterpart in the dustbin of autocratic rule.

It is thus that when he delivered his February 11 speech that he seemed energized.

"...By stepping down, President Mubarak responded to the Egyptian people's hunger for change," he asserted. "...Egyptians have made it clear that nothing less than genuine democracy will carry the day."

He continued: "The United States will continue to be a friend and partner to Egypt. We stand ready to provide whatever assistance is necessary—and asked for—to pursue a credible transition to a democracy... We [are seeing] a new generation emerge—a generation that uses their own creativity and talent and technology to call for a government that represent[s] their hopes and not their fears; a government that is responsive to their boundless aspirations... This is the power of human dignity, and it can never be denied. Egyptians have inspired us, and they've done so by putting the lie to the idea that justice is best gained through violence. For in Egypt, it was the moral force of nonviolence ... that bent the arc of history toward justice once more. And while the sights and sounds that we heard were entirely Egyptian, we can't help but hear the echoes of history—echoes from Germans tearing down a wall, Indonesian students taking to the streets, Gandhi leading his people down the path of justice. As Martin Luther King said in celebrating the birth of a new nation in Ghana while trying to perfect his own, 'There is something in the soul that cries out for freedom.' Those were the cries that came from Tahrir Square, and the entire world has taken note... The word 'Tahrir' means liberation. It is a word that speaks to that something in our souls that cries out for freedom. And forevermore it will remind us of the Egyptian people—of what they did, of the things that they stood for, and how they changed their country, and in doing so changed the world."[117]

Egyptian "Democracy" in Action

On February 12, the day after the "moral force of non-violence bent the arc of history toward justice," the new interim leadership in Egypt—the Supreme Council of Egyptian Armed Forces—announced the imposition of travel bans on many of Mubarak's ministers. It was now time for "justice"—in other words, revenge.

On February 13, it dissolved the parliament and suspended the Constitution.

On February 14, it issued a communiqué warning against labor or other strikes.

On February 15, Amr Mosa resigned his post as Secretary-General of the Arab League to run in the upcoming Egyptian presidential election, and the Muslim Brotherhood announced that it was forming the Freedom and Justice Party to run in the parliamentary elections.

On February 17, it detained a number of leading figures from the former regime, among them the interior, housing, and tourism ministers.

On February 21, it temporarily lifted a media blackout it had imposed, in order to play up a visit by British Prime Minister David Cameron—the first world leader to visit post-Mubarak Egypt.

On March 3, Prime Minister Ahmed Shafik resigned, preempting mass protests against him that were scheduled to take place the following day.

On March 5, protesters raided buildings of the State Security Investigations Service (SSI), claiming they needed to get hold of documentation of torture and other crimes committed against citizens during Mubarak's tenure. Ten days later, the agency was dissolved. That evening, thousands of angry Muslims, screaming *"allahu akbar,"* descended upon a Coptic Christian village about 20 miles from Cairo, setting two churches on fire and terrorizing private homes. The mob prevented fire fighters from entering the area. The army, which initially refused to get involved, eventually sent in three tanks to disperse the crowd, but left when a Muslim elder told them everything was under control. The end result was that a curfew was imposed on the Christian residents of the village.

On March 8, hundreds of Egyptian women were harassed by their "freedom-seeking" male counterparts for attempting to celebrate International Women's Day with a "Million Women's March" in Cairo. The aim of the march was to express a desire to take an active role in post-Mubarak Egypt. The aim of the male counter-protest was to object to allowing women to run for the presidency in the new constitution.

As the women began to march, the men surrounded and groped them, chanting, "The people want to bring down women!"[118]

On March 23, the cabinet enacted legislation banning protests and strikes. According to this law, anyone organizing or calling for a protest would be jailed and/or heavily fined.

On March 29, Egypt's new foreign minister, Nabil al-Arabi, called for renewed diplomatic relations with Iran, in what he called "a move to turn over a new leaf."

On April 1, thousands of demonstrators at Tahrir Square demanded that the Supreme Council move faster to dismantle all vestiges of Mubarak's regime.

On April 5, the Supreme Council arrested Mubrak's housing minister.

On April 8, hundreds of thousands of demonstrators took to Tahrir Square again, demanding the ouster of all remaining regime figures, as well as the public prosecutor, for not speeding up the process of going after former officials.

On April 9, the Supreme Council ordered soldiers to use force against protesters camped out at Tahrir Square.

On April 12, Mubarak was hospitalized in Sharm el-Sheikh. According to some reports, he had suffered a heart attack during questioning by prosecutors for charges of corruption. The Egyptian prosecutors denied this allegation, asserting that he was well enough to undergo continued interrogation while in the hospital.

On April 13, the Egyptian Prosecutor General ordered that Mubarak and his two children, Alaa and Gamal, be detained for 15 days. According to a statement published on the Egyptian Attorney General's Facebook page, the arrest warrant for the three Mubaraks was issued after the prosecution presented the charges of corruption and criminal behavior during the Tahrir Square protests.

On April 16, the Egyptian supreme administrative court ordered that Mubarak's National Democratic Party be dissolved and its assets handed over to the new government.

On April 18, Iran appointed its first ambassador to Egypt in 30 years.

Relations between the two countries had been severed by the Islamic Republic when Egyptian President Anwar Sadat allied himself with the West. Now, following the toppling of Sadat's successor, warm ties could happily be resumed.

On April 21, Mubarak's name was removed from all public places in Egypt.

On April 24, the Egyptian Prosecutor's office ordered the arrest of former Egyptian Energy Minister Sameh Fahmy and six other officials, all of whom would be put on trial for exporting natural gas to Israel at lower prices than those of the market, and for exploiting public funds accrued from the gas deal.

Meanwhile, Egyptian authorities ordered that Mubarak be transferred from Sharm el-Sheikh to the Tora prison hospital in Cairo at a date to be determined.

On April 25, a Pew poll revealed that Egyptians were distrustful of the United States and wanted to renegotiate the peace treaty with Israel that had been in effect for three decades.

On April 27, the gas pipeline from Egypt to Israel was attacked by unknown armed saboteurs.[119] It was inoperable for several weeks while being repaired.

On April 30, the Muslim Brotherhood formed the Freedom and Justice Party to run in the elections, then slated for September.[120] This was an open bid to gain a parliamentary majority in the body from which it had been banned by the former Egyptian constitution for being religion-based. To get around this restriction, in previous elections, the Brotherhood fielded candidates as "independents." With Mubarak and his constitution gone, the Islamist organization was now able to run openly, without hiding its agenda or its candidates.

On May 1, Egyptian Foreign Minister Nabil al-Arabi called on the United States to recognize a Palestinian state, ahead of the Egyptian-brokered reconciliation between the Fatah-led Palestinian Authority and its openly terrorist Islamist counterpart, Hamas.

On May 4, PA President Mahmoud Abbas and Hamas leader Khaled Mashaal met in Cairo to endorse the Egyptian-brokered deal to end the four-year rift between the secular Fatah group and its Islamist rival.

On May 8, at least a dozen people were killed and more than 200 wounded during violent clashes on the part of Muslims against Christians outside a Cairo church, spurred by rumors that a Christian woman who converted to Islam was being held there against her will. This led to public pleas from Coptic Christians for international protection.

On May 24, it was announced that Mubarak and his sons would be tried for the deaths of anti-government protesters.

On May 28, the new Egyptian authorities lifted a four-year-old blockade of Gaza, easing travel restrictions on its 1.5 million residents and bolstering its terrorist, Hamas-led government. On May 30, a senior member of the Egyptian military admitted that virginity tests had been performed on protesters arrested during the March 8 women's rally in Cairo. The official defended the practice by saying that the tests were done to prevent the women from later claiming they had been raped by their interrogators.[121]

On June 28, Egyptian security forces attacked protestors in Tahrir Square.

On July 1, tens of thousands of protesters gathered in Tahrir Square and other places in Egypt to express frustration with the military for the "slow pace of change." This demonstration was called the "Friday of Retribution."

On July 8, hundreds of thousands of protesters gathered and began to camp out at Tahrir Square and other places in Egypt, demanding immediate prosecution of former government officials. This demonstration was called the "Friday of Determination."

On July 15, tens of thousands of Islamists descended upon Tahrir Square, in a bid to outrank and outnumber the more secular demonstrators camped out there, and to demand recognition of their growing political power. Members of the Muslim Brotherhood, extremist Salafists and others who believed in having Egypt governed by Sharia law joined together to demonstrate and pray for the election of Hazem Salah Abu Ismail, a Salafist sympathetic to the Muslim Brotherhood, as the next president of Egypt. This demonstration was called the "Friday of the last ultimatum."

On July 23—the anniversary of the 1952 military coup against Egypt's monarchy—an estimated 5,000 protestors marched from Defense Ministry headquarters in Abbasseya to Tahrir Square to demonstrate against military rule. Egyptian security forces tried to disperse the gathering by firing shots in the air. Residents of the area threw rocks and Molotov cocktails at the protesters.

On August 1, members of the military attacked protesters camped out in Tahrir Square. Wielding electrified batons and screaming *"allahu akbar,"* they tore down tents and arrested several of the tents' occupants. Many Egyptian onlookers joined in the ranting of *"allahu akbar,"* cheering the soldiers' violence against the tent campers.

On August 3, Egyptians watched the opening of the trial against Mubarak, his sons, and other top officials on state television. The charges: corruption and the premeditated murder of citizens who had participated in the protests against his reign. The latter charge carried the death penalty. Gleeful citizens gloated over the fact that their former president—who pleaded not guilty to the accusations—was wheeled into the courtroom on a hospital bed inside of a cage.

On August 6, more protesters gathered in Tahrir Square were brutally attacked by police and security forces.

On August 14, youth protest leader Asmaa Mahfous was arrested for calling the Egyptian military a "council of dogs." Two presidential candidates, Mohamed ElBaradei and Ayman Nour, came to her defense. Eventually, the charges against her were dropped.[122]

On August 18, an apparently al-Qaeda-linked terrorist attack in southern Israel, near the Egyptian border, resulted in many casualties, among them five Egyptian soldiers caught in the crossfire. The multi-pronged assault involved shootings, a mortar attack and a suicide bombing, perpetrated by Palestinians disguised in Egyptian army uniforms. In spite of an apology on the part of the Israeli government for the deaths of the soldiers (who it is not even clear were killed by IDF fire), Egypt recalled its ambassador from Israel. Egyptian masses, shouting *"allahu akbar,"* began demonstrating in front of the Israeli Embassy in Cairo, demanding an end to the peace treaty with Israel.

On September 9—the "Friday of Correcting the Path," tens of thousands of politically secular Egyptians staged demonstrations across the country demanding the ouster of the Interior Minister, the stopping of military trials for civilians conducted by the now ruling Supreme Council, and the severing of diplomatic ties with Israel.

As night fell, a few thousand of these "reformists" made their way to the Israeli Embassy in Cairo, chanting *"allahu akbar"* and "End the treaty," while security forces stood by passively. Then, they began sledge-hammering the outside wall until it collapsed. As night fell—with no security forces stopping them—dozens stormed through the building. Terrorized embassy staffers who were holed up in one of the rooms reported on their plight via phone to Prime Minister Benjamin Netanyahu as the lynch mob tore through the building in search of Israeli blood to spill. At around midnight, Netanyahu called President Obama, and begged him to intervene. This Obama finally did, just in time to spare the lives of the young diplomats at the embassy. The following day, op-eds in the Israeli media were rife with comparisons to the 1979 US Embassy takeover in Tehran, as on the other hand did the Iranian press, which referred to the incident as the siege on the "den of Zionists."

On September 10, Israeli Ambassador to Egypt Yitzhak Levanon and his staff fled Cairo and flew home. The Israeli government then began a series of discussions with Egypt's ruling council to try to patch things up.

On September 11—the tenth anniversary of the World Trade Center bombings—there was a sense, according to PBS Newshour's Margaret Warner, of "the enduring appeal of anti-US sentiment and terrorism in Egypt, which was the 20th century incubator of Islamic jihadism and the birthplace of Ayman al-Zawahiri, the new chief of al-Qaeda." The concern among the people in the street whom she interviewed, she noted, was more about their not knowing how to live without a leader than about how to govern themselves.

On September 30, a Coptic Christian church undergoing renovation in a village in Aswan was attacked by thousands of Muslims. The ostensible reason for this was that the church leaders had ignored their building permit, which stipulated that the structure could display no Christian symbols (i.e. crosses, bells, and domes)—something that would "offend" Muslims. The angry mob began using tools and other objects to destroy the property, ultimately doing it with gasoline and setting it ablaze. The thugs then proceeded to loot and torch a number of nearby homes occupied by Copts. SCAF forces basically stood by and did nothing. The governor of Aswan subsequently blamed the Christians for the incident, because he said it was they who had violated their permits.

On October 3, the SCAF appointed a censor for the Egyptian media, sparking op-ed writers to leave their columns blank the following day.

On October 4, the head of the Egypt section at the US Security Council and the First Secretary of the US Embassy in Cairo paid a visit to the headquarters of the Muslim Brotherhood's Freedom and Justice party to meet with its secretary-general. This was a goodwill gesture offered by the Obama Administration, which realized that the formerly banned group would undoubtedly garner much support in the parliamentary elections, and would emerge as a force to be reckoned with and therefore would need to be befriended.

On October 5, hundreds of demonstrators marched to Tahrir Square demanding that the SCAF step up the transfer of its power to an elected government and president.

On October 7—the "Second Friday of Anger"—a demonstration erupted, following prayer services, against the SCAF's imposing of stricter measures against the population. Among these was a renewal and strengthening of the previous Emergency Law (enabling arrests at will), media censorship and military trials for civilians.

On October 9, in response to the destruction of the church in Aswan, hundreds of Coptic Christians, joined by Muslim sympathizers, held a sit-in outside of the TV station in Maspiro, calling for the dissolution of the SCAF, the resignation of its chief, Mohamed Tantawi, and the dismissal of the governor of Aswan. But as they approached, they were attacked by soldiers and police, who sprayed them with tear gas, rammed into them with army vehicles and shot at them. Twenty-seven demonstrators were killed and more than 200 wounded. The majority of the casualties were sustained by Copts. During the riots, the army also stormed the TV station and cut off its broadcasts. Meanwhile, the state-run press called on the public to protect the army from the Copts.

On November 1, the Egyptian deputy prime minister released a draft of the new constitution. The "constitutional principles document" gave the SCAF the sole right to oversee all matters related to the military, enabling it to be above civilian and judicial oversight.

On November 19, thousands of demonstrators descended on Tahrir Square, in what was a renewal of the revolution, this time against the SCAF. The thousands of demonstrators were demanding the resignation of Tantawi and that the SCAF relinquish control over the country to a civilian government. Many of the protesters were Islamists organized by the Muslim Brotherhood. Security forces used tear gas to disperse the crowd, but to no avail.

On November 20, security forces began to force demonstrators out of Tahrir Square, but they returned in greater numbers later in the day. Rioting erupted and continued until late at night, with security forces beating up and shooting at the demonstrators. At least two dozen were killed and nearly two thousand wounded.

On November 21, similar demonstrations were held throughout Egypt, in solidarity with the Tahrir Square protest. Prime Minister Essam Sharaf and his cabinet tendered their resignations.

On November 25, Tantawi enraged the public by appointing Kamal Ganzori—who had served in the Mubarak regime in the late 1990s—prime minister. In response, anti-SCAF demonstrations were held in cities across the country.

On November 28, the first of the several-stage parliamentary elections was held. The Muslim Brotherhood ignored bans on campaigning at the polling stations with impunity.

During the first half of December, protesters continued a mass sit-in outside of a government building near Tahrir Square that had been launched in response to the appointment of Ganzouri as prime minister.

On December 10, Senate Foreign Relations Committee Chairman John Kerry—among the first American politicians to urge Mubarak to resign—met with three top Muslim Brotherhood officials in Cairo. US Ambassador to Egypt Anne Patterson accompanied him to the meeting, during which the Democrat from Massachusetts told his hosts that he was not surprised by their electoral success so far. In turn, they made assurances that America could count on them to uphold democratic principles.

On December 16, the SCAF took forceful action to quell the sit-in—later issuing a statement blaming the protesters for the ensuing violence. The events of the day were described by Al Jazeera's Rawya Rageh as "ugly." She reported from Cairo that there were "men in uniform perched on the rooftops of buildings, throwing whatever they can lay their hands on on protesters, including sheets of glass, bottles, rocks, and at one point even furniture. Very unpleasant scenes, including some of these soldiers gesturing obscenely towards the protesters, and one of them even at one point urinating on the protesters gathered below."

On December 17, the army clashed with the protesters again. During the day's violence, the death-toll reached 11.

On December 19, parliament members and Muslim Brotherhood representatives organized a sit-in outside of the Supreme Court to protest the SCAF violence and to demand that the leadership of the country be handed over to a civilian president by the end of January. Meanwhile, one SCAF member denied that any violence was used during the protests. And retired general Abdel Moneim Kato, an advisor in the government's "Morale Department," gave an interview to the *Al Shorouk* newspaper, in which he called the protesters delinquents "who deserve to be thrown into Hitler's ovens."

In response to the escalation of violence, US Secretary of State Hillary Clinton urged the SCAF generals to respect human rights. In a speech she gave at Georgetown University, she also expressed "shock" at the fact that "women are being beaten and humiliated in the same streets where they risked their lives for the revolution only a few short months ago."

On December 20, thousands of Egyptian women took to the streets to protest abuse at the hands of security forces. Again, troops attacked the rest of the masses with tear gas and gunfire.

On December 23, tens of thousands of demonstrators—among them university students and Salafist activists—descended on Tahrir Square to protest SCAF violence. Several thousand in other cities held similar anti-military marches.

Thousands of others held a counter-demonstration, defending the military as the only stabilizing force in the country.

On December 29, Egyptian government forces raided the offices of 17 NGOs, among them the Arab Center for Independence of the Judiciary and the Legal Profession, the Budgetary and Human Rights Observatory, and the Washington, DC-based National Democratic Institute, International Republican Institute and Freedom House—for not having proper "licensing and registration." Meanwhile, Tantawi ordered an investigation into "allegations" of violence on the part of security forces against protesters. Since it was also Tantawi who ordered the security forces to use violence against the protesters—or who allowed them to do so after the fact—this move was clearly aimed at showing the administration in Washington that justice was being served, and democratic processes were underway under SCAF auspices.

On January 1, hundreds of thousands of Egyptians took to the streets to honor those killed during the recent clashes between protesters and the military, chanting the same revolutionary slogans against the SCAF that previously had been aimed at Mubarak.

On January 3, *The New York Times* reported that, in the lead-up to the final results of the Egyptian elections for the lower house of parliament, the Obama Administration "has begun to reverse decades of mistrust and hostility as it seeks to forge closer ties with an organization [the Muslim Brotherhood] once viewed as irreconcilably opposed to United States interests."

According to the article, "The administration's overtures—including high-level meetings in recent weeks—constitute a historic shift in a foreign policy held by successive American administrations that steadfastly supported the autocratic government of President Hosni Mubarak in part out of concern for the Brotherhood's Islamist ideology and historic ties to militants." This, the piece went on, was partly an "acknowledgment of the new political reality" in Egypt and the rest of the Middle East "as Islamist groups come to power." But it is also a reflection on the Obama Administration's "growing acceptance of the Brotherhood's repeated assurances that its lawmakers want to build a modern democracy that will respect individual freedoms, free markets and international commitments, including Egypt's treaty with Israel."

On January 10, the third stage of elections for the lower house of the Egyptian parliament began. During the day, renowned Egyptian (female) author Lamees Gaber gave an interview to Al-Hayat TV in which she criticized the public's treatment of the military. She said that her countrymen "have become fed up with the revolution," and she went as far as to put down a woman who was beaten by security forces in Tahrir Square on December 17, asserting that "burned books [like those destroyed in a fire at the Insitut d'Égypt during the December riots] are more important than a woman's honor." This is in spite of the fact that there is video footage of the incident, during which the woman has been shoved to the ground and is being stomped on by soldiers, while what appears to be her chador has been pulled over her head, exposing her bra and bare stomach. The image of the young woman—like that of Neda Soltan in Iran—instantly hit the Internet and became an icon of the anti-military demonstrations in Egypt. Meanwhile, former US President Jimmy Carter—in Egypt to monitor the final round of parliamentary elections—met with Tantawi and other SCAF leaders.

On January 11, Carter gave an interview to *The New York Times*, in which he described his discussions with Tantawi and expressed his views on the role the military would play in the post-Mubarak era.

"'If the civilian leadership decided to give the SCAF immunity from prosecution, say, for the death of the people in Tahrir Square over the last few months, I would have no objection to that,' Mr. Carter said. Protecting the military budget from full civilian scrutiny might be another point where civilian political leaders could compromise... He[also] praised the Obama administration for its decision to accept the outcome of Egyptian elections even if they have been dominated by the Muslim Brotherhood... He contrasted that choice with Washington's refusal to recognize the 2006 victory of the militant Islamist group Hamas in elections in the Palestinian territories. 'A dramatic improvement,' he said. 'Improvement is not a strong enough word.'"[123]

On January 12, one of the headquarters of the Muslim Brotherhood's Freedom and Justice Party was torched by disgruntled voters, when its candidate for the "workers' seat" in parliament beat the candidate connected with the dissolved National Democratic Party. The arsons also set three shops on fire and physically assaulted a number of the winning candidate's supporters.

On January 13, protesters marched in Tahrir Square, demanding retribution for the deaths of fellow protesters in the revolution, calling for a quick transition to civilian rule, and demanding that natural gas exports to Israel be stopped.

On January 14, former International Atomic Energy Agency head Mohammed ElBaradei withdrew his bid to run for president, attributing his move to the fact that the "old regime [had] not been changed."

On January 20, the polls closed on the final state of the elections for the People's Assembly, the lower house of the Egyptian Parliament. Several hours later, the Islamists emerged victorious, having garnered nearly three quarters of the seats. The Assembly is made up of 498 elected parliament members and an additional 10 appointed by the SCAF. The Muslim Brotherhood's Freedom and Justice Party came in first; the Salafist Al-Nur Party (even more extreme than the Muslim Brotherhood) came in second; and the liberal Wafd Party and Egyptian Bloc came in third and fourth.

Not Confused by the Facts

Upon learning of Egypt's election results, Obama immediately phoned Tantawi "to reaffirm the close partnership between the United States and Egypt and to underscore the United States' support for Egypt's transition to democracy."

According to a White House press release, the president "welcomed the historic seating of the lower house of Egypt's Parliament and offered his congratulations to the Egyptian people on taking this important step towards democracy."

He also "reinforced the necessity of upholding universal principles and emphasized the important role that civil society, including non-governmental organizations, have in a democratic society... and underscored that non-governmental organizations should be able to operate freely." (This was in reference to the raids on, and shutting down of, the Washington-based NGOs by the SCAF, due to "improper registration." Subsequently, American NGO staffers would be arrested and not allowed to leave Egypt.)

After talking about "Egypt's economic situation and the ongoing discussions between Egypt and the International Monetary Fund on an economic program that can garner the broad support of the Egyptian people," Obama and Tantawi "discussed the importance of continuing to cooperate closely on counter-terrorism and regional security issues." Finally, the two leaders "agreed to remain in close touch in the months ahead as Egypt continues its transition to democracy."

Three things did not seem to enter Obama's mind during this congratulatory chat with the "democracy-prone" field marshal. The first is that Tantawi's main interest is and always has been ensuring that the Supreme Council of the Armed Forces holds on to as much civilian power as it possibly can—not overseeing his country's shift to some form of Western democracy. To this end, the SCAF has worked out a deal with the Muslim Brotherhood, according to which it would retain a degree of leadership status, and serve as the country's liaison with the West.

The second is that the Muslim Brotherhood—whatever fantasies its Western apologists have about its intentions and ideology—is itself a conduit of terrorism, not an organization aimed at stamping out the phenomenon. Though it espouses the belief that the world can be sub-jugated to Islamic law (sharia) through a powerful global network of mosques, NGOs, and other forms of societal infiltration without the use of bombs, its goal is no different from that of the more blatantly extremist Salafists—or from that of its patron Iran.

The third thing Obama failed to take into account is the coalition that the Brotherhood is cooking up with the Salafists, who came in in second place in the parliamentary elections. Such a union will create not only a power base that is impenetrable politically, but one that will make Mubarak's autocratic regime look like Disneyland for the Egyptian people who gleefully watch him being wheeled into his trial on a gurney enclosed by a cage.

Indeed, says pundit and *Jerusalem Post* columnist Caroline Glick, the situation as it has emerged is "bad news for women and for non-Muslims. Egypt's Coptic Christians have been under continuous attack by Muslim Brotherhood and Salafist supporters since Mubarak was de-posed. Their churches, homes and businesses have been burned, looted and destroyed. Their wives and daughters have been raped. The military massacred them when they dared to protest their persecution."[124]

Outside observers from the school of Jimmy Carter's and John Ker-ry—as well as the left-leaning media—who cling to the fantasy that all of this nasty stuff will disappear once Egypt has ratified its constitution, says Glick, "fail to recognize...that the Islamic fundamentalists now in charge of Egypt don't need a constitution to implement their tyranny. All they require is what they already have—a public awareness of their political power and their partnership with the military."[125]

Epilogue

On February 4, NFL fans across the United States were doggedly preparing for the following day's event of the year—Super Bowl XLVI. The more affluent among them had purchased exorbitantly priced tickets and reserved hotel rooms in Indianapolis, in order to see for themselves whether the New York Giants would put on a repeat performance of their stunning last-minute victory over the New England Patriots four years earlier. Slightly less fortunate Americans had reserved tables at sports bars or invited friends to watch the game on TV, with buckets of Kentucky Fried Chicken, bowls of popcorn, and beer on ice in bathtubs. As it would turn out, those rooting for the Patriots would wind up having to go back to work on Monday, praying for better luck next time.

Across the ocean, Egyptians of all stripes were also engaged in sports-related activities. But the soccer match that sparked them had already taken place a week earlier. When the game in Port Said between rival teams al-Masry and al-Ahly was over, with the latter emerging the winner, riots the likes of which have not been seen in soccer history erupted. The violence—that left 74 dead and hundreds wounded—began in a curious way, to put it mildly. As soon as the match was over, scores of fans from the *winning* team began to vent their rage at the losers.

Nor did the carnage stop there. Immediately after the outbreak, which involved rock-throwing, knifing, shooting, stampeding, and setting fire to the stadium, the rest of the Egyptian populace followed suit. Treating the event as part of the wider revolution (and, indeed, many of the al-Ahly fans were at the forefront of the anti-Mubarak and then anti-SCAF protests), the Tahrir Square "democracy seekers" put the lie to Western media speculation that the bloody clashes were merely another example of soccer hooliganism. Proof of this lay in the fact thousands more Egyptians were seriously wounded in demonstrations that grew out of the sports disaster.

On that same February 4, while Americans were preparing for the next day's Super Bowl and Egyptians were gathering rocks and other weapons to prepare for the next day's round of soccer-spurred street fighting, Iranians were being treated to another round of regime indoctrination. This took the form of an article published on the Iranian Web site, Alef, written by one of Supreme Leader Ayatollah Ali Khamenei's strategists, Alireza Forghani. The article, titled "Jurisprudential Reasons for Israel's Destruction," was then posted on other sites, among them the Fars News Agency. As Reza Kahlili, who exposed the piece in World Net Daily, pointed out, this was a sign that its content was endorsed by the Iranian regime. Since it was completely in keeping with the public statements Khamenei had made the day before the article came out, it is clear that Kahlili was correct.

In a two-hour televised speech marking the 33rd anniversary of the toppling of the Shah, the Supreme Leader vowed to remove the "cancerous tumor" Israel, if it should launch a pre-emptive military attack on

Iranian nuclear installations. His threats were obviously in reference to reports emerging from the Netanyahu government that such a strike was in the cards, and to an acknowledgement by Defense Secretary Leon Panetta that there was a "strong likelihood" of an Israeli attack sometime in the spring.

"From now on," Khamenei announced, "in any place, if any nation or group confronts the Zionist regime, we will endorse and we will help." He then officially confirmed what everybody had known all along about Iran's financial and other backing of terrorist organizations all over the world, by taking credit for the "victories" against of Hizbullah in Lebanon in 2006 and Hamas in Gaza two years later.

According to the World Net Daily account of Forghani's piece, though some Shi'ite jurists say that the Muslim duty of "primary jihad" against the infidels can only take place when the Mahdi (the 12th or Hidden Iman) returns, it is both legally viable and a religious imperative for all Muslims to engage in "defensive jihad" when Islam is under attack.

The time is now, Forghani insisted, because "in order to attack Iran, Israel needs the approval and assistance of America, and *under the current passive climate in the United States* [emphasis added], the opportunity must not be lost to wipe out Israel before it attacks Iran."

He then went on to be specific about "Ground Zero" targets in Jerusalem, Tel Aviv, and Haifa, as well as the airports and communication infrastructures, even detailing which Iranian missiles have the capability of destroying the Jewish state and killing all its inhabitants—an undertaking, he claimed, that would take less than nine minutes.

Finally, Forghani asserted that Khamenei believes that the United States, too, must not only be defeated, but annihilated as well.

This did not appear to shake Obama's conviction about the proper response to Iran's nuclear weapons program, however. On Super Bowl Sunday (February 5), Obama gave a pre-game interview with NBC's

Matt Lauer, in which he reiterated his favored path in dealing with the Islamic Republic: diplomacy.

Contradicting what Panetta had said about a likely Israeli strike on Iran's nuclear facilities, Obama said, "I don't think Israel has made a decision. I think they, like us, think Iran has to stand down their nuclear weapons program... [and] We are going to make sure we work in lock step and work to resolve this, hopefully diplomatically... Our preferred solution is diplomatic, we're going to keep on pushing on that front ... [but] I've been very clear that we're going to do everything we can to prevent Iran from getting a nuclear weapon and creating an arms race, a nuclear arms race, in a volatile region." He then said that international sanctions have been working.

This assertion was as delusional as the view that the "Arab Spring" is the harbinger of budding democracies across the Middle East.

In fact, sanctions have done nothing to halt Iran's nuclear program; if anything, they have served to strengthen the Islamic Republic's resolve to step up its uranium enrichment and ballistic missile warhead production. Nor have Obama's assurances that "all options are still on the table" deterred the regime in Tehran one iota. On the contrary, while Khamenei clearly takes Israel's warnings seriously—which is why he announced, through Forghani, that preemptive jihad need not wait until the return of the 12th imam—he does not view America as anything but weak.

And well might he hold such a view.

From the moment that Obama took office, he made it clear to radical Muslims the world over that his main objective was to promise them that they had nothing to fear from the United States. And he has kept that promise beyond expectations. His Cairo speech, in which he spelled this out in no uncertain terms before an audience of Muslim Brotherhood champions, was among many gestures aimed at disavowing American exceptionalism, superiority—and, above all, power—while stressing the strengths of the Third World.

Other such moves on his administration's part would have been funny if they hadn't been so sad. For example, Obama informed NASA that one of its top priorities must be to make Muslims feel good about themselves and their contributions to science and math.

And Homeland Security Secretary Janet Napolitano replaced the word "terrorism" with "man-caused" disasters. This she did, she told *Der Spiegel* in March 2009, "in order to move away from the politics of fear toward a policy of being prepared for all risks that can occur." When translated from "Obama-speak," this means "Let's not offend Muslims."

But since Obama and his gang have been shouting from the rooftops that most Muslims are not terrorists—or even radical in their views or practices—it was revealing that such liberties were taken with the English language. The question is: on whose behalf were they taken? Peaceful Muslims? Terrorists who just happen to believe in Islam?

Nor are the likes of Khamenei and Ahmadinejad the only ones laughing all the way to the bank over the Obama Administration's handling of the "delicate" issue of jihad—one whose message has been spreading like wildfire since Mohamed Bouazizi, the Tunisian street vendor, lit the match. One by one, every country in the Middle East has fallen or is about to fall to the radical Islamists, thanks to a lot of help from their friends in the White House and State Department.

As Middle East analyst Martin Sherman pointed out, such an "approach to international relations—cold-shouldering democratic allies and kowtowing to dictatorial adversaries—has not only been distinctly counterintuitive but disastrously counterproductive."[126]

To illustrate, let's start with Tunisia, where the "Arab Spring" was ignited. Its first "democratic" elections were held on October 23, 2011. The biggest winner was the formerly banned Islamist party Ennahda. This was a source of great jubilation both to the populace, who were appalled by the over-secular flavor of the Ben-Ali regime, and to the merchants of Islamic dress and headgear, now certain to be sold in bulk. In fact, business in scarves and hijabs has been booming since then.

In Egypt, as we have seen, the Muslim Brotherhood and Salafists are the victors in the post-Mubarak era.

In Yemen, too, Islamists have taken advantage of the leadership vacuum—as a result of Saleh's having left the country—to establish a secure power base with which to dominate. Different groups, such as Islah (the Yemeni branch of the Muslim Brotherhood), the Salafis, and the jihadist movements linked to AQAP (al-Qaeda in the Arabian Peninsula), have been mobilizing to take over when elections are held.

In Libya, where Obama "led behind" the NATO forces to help over-throw Muammar Gaddafi, radical Islamic groups—backed, apparently, by al-Qaeda (the key anti-regime oppositionists alongside the United States and Europe)—are gearing up to take over. Considering the gleeful and hungry way that Lybian "Arab Springers" sodomized Gaddafi and tore him limb from limb when they uncovered his hiding place, it is clear that what lies ahead is not pretty.

In Bahrain, where protests against the Sunni King are being held by the mostly Shi'ite population, the "Arab Spring" has been less successful, so far, than in some neighboring countries. This is in spite of the fact that Iran, which is Shi'ite, is championing its brethren against the monarchy. Though the Bahraini rebels deny being puppets of the Iranian regime, if and when the monarchy falls, they will be what Brig.-Gen. Qassem Sulei-mani, the commander of Iran's Revolutionary Guards Corps Jerusalem Brigade, "subject to the control of the Islamic Republic of Iran and its ideas." Suleimani was referring to the Iraqi people and Jordanians when he made that statement at a student symposium in Tehran in January 2012, but he knew what he was talking about with regard to the region as a whole. And he can take credit, along with Obama, for what has happened in Iraq since the United States withdrew its troops in December 2011. With the vacuum Obama was in such a hurry to create, it is now Iran that is "capturing the hearts and minds" of the Iraqi people.

And this brings us to Syria. There, the "Arab Spring" protesters are being slaughtered by Bashar Assad, the dictator who has proven as ruthless as his late father, Hafez—infamous for the massacring of his own people.

As was the case during the student uprisings in Iran after Ahmadinejad stole the election in June 2009, the Obama administration turned a (falsely sympathetic) blind eye to the opposition forces in Syria. The only move so far that the State Department has taken in response to the daily carnage that Assad is carrying out is to shut down the US Embassy in Damascus, and to urge the dictator to stop killing his people. Meanwhile, as he has done in relation to the regime in Tehran—as opposed to the other Middle East leaders who were American allies—Obama has chosen the "diplomatic" route where this sworn enemy is concerned.

To make matters worse, the country he approached to mediate between the United States and Syria was Turkey—a former pro-Western democracy that shunned its long-time allegiance with America to side with its Islamist brethren.

And well everyone else may follow suit, if America's message to the world is that it has opted out of being a superpower, and chosen instead to "lead from behind." Even those countries, like Saudi Arabia, that have not yet abandoned their "friendship" with the United States, due to its fear of Iranian hegemony, is running scared.

The rest of us should be equally afraid of the "Arab Spring" and America's response to it.

In the first place, whatever social ills and lack of freedoms spurred "democracy seekers" to take to the streets, it was not they who toppled their autocrats. Those activists were neither numerous enough nor sufficiently organized to make a difference. What got the masses going, as *National Review*'s Andrew McCarthy explains, was not the repression of regimes against the people, but the repression of those regimes against Islam. "If you understand this," he writes, "you understand why Western beliefs about the Arab Spring—and the Western conceit that the death of one tyranny must herald the birth of liberty—have always been a delusion."[127]

As such, the "Arab Spring" poses a serious threat to the very ideals that the United States and Europe insist are at its root. And basing foreign policy on such fantasies is serving to hasten the spread of the most pernicious form of extremism since the Third Reich—only this time it is equipping itself with long-range nuclear missiles.

Secondly, though many pundits have been asserting that the "Arab Spring"—albeit violent and of uncertain outcome—is a necessary precursor to a process whose ultimate aim is liberty, they also quietly concede that it will take a very long time for this ostensible "universal" dream to come true. The example that has been bandied about most frequently is the French Revolution. But, since none of us will be alive in 100 years to evaluate the accuracy of the metaphor, it is about as helpful to American foreign policy as sanctions have been in preventing Iran from acquiring nuclear weapons.

It is possible, perhaps even likely, that the point of no return has passed where Iranian nuclear weapons are concerned. This does not mean that America has to roll over and play dead, however. Nor should Obama behave like his eerily similar predecessor, Jimmy Carter, and actively assist the anti-Western forces in their endeavor. It certainly doesn't warrant the massive cut in defense spending that Obama has been pushing for. After all, *he* may be against warfare, but America's bloodthirsty enemies are decidedly not.

If history has taught us anything is that it is never too late to reassert American values and the will to live by them. But this requires the willingness to die for them, as well.

Which brings us to a very different election from those that are taking place in the Middle East as a result of the "Arab Spring."

When Americans go to the polls in November 2012, they will have a serious choice to make: whether to adhere to Obama's dim view of American greatness, or to reclaim their place as beacons for the rest of the world—and as saviors for those who would emulate that light if given a genuine chance to do so.

Obama still has the opportunity to alter his view and policies. But rather than admitting to their failures, he has been clinging to them for dear life. That was certainly not the American dream his forefathers had in mind when they wrote the Constitution. Nor should it be that of any citizen of the United States today—and above all, not that of the commander-in-chief.

Notes

1   The July 1999 demonstrations began peacefully, but ended tragically. Police
    raided a Tehran University dorm. In the clash, a student was killed. This
    sparked a week of rioting throughout the country, leaving a few people dead
    and hundreds injured. After that, over 1,000 people were detained by Islamic
    authorities. Dozens of students "disappeared," and their whereabouts are un-
    known to this day. The 2003 demonstrations took place in June. Thousands
    of student protesters stormed the streets of Tehran, but the regime quickly
    quelled the rebellion.

2   Moussavi, who had by now become, almost unwittingly, the leader of the
    grass-roots counterrevolution, was among the opposition leaders who boy-
    cotted Ahmadinejad's swearing-in ceremony on August 5.

3   She made this statement at a joint news conference in Niagara Falls, Ontario,
    with Canadian Foreign Affairs Minister Lawrence Cannon.

4   The speech, titled "A New Beginning," was delivered by the president on June
    4, 2009 at Cairo University. In it, Obama praised Islam, extending friend-

ship to the Muslim world. In relation to Iran he said, "Rather than remain trapped in the past, I've made it clear to Iran's leaders and people that my country is prepared to move forward. The question now is not what Iran is against, but rather what future it wants to build. I recognize it will be hard to overcome decades of mistrust, but we will proceed with courage, rectitude, and resolve. There will be many issues to discuss between our two countries, and we are willing to move forward without preconditions on the basis of mutual respect."

5   The P5+1 refers to the five permanent UN Security Council members (Britain, China, France, Russia and the United States) plus Germany, whose stated aim is to strengthen the Nuclear Non-Proliferation Treaty. According to Obama's statement on October 1, 2009 about the meeting of the P5+1 in Geneva with Iranian representatives, "Iran must take concrete steps to build confidence that its nuclear program will serve peaceful purposes—steps that meet Iran's obligations under multiple UN Security Council resolutions."

6   This was confirmed both by the reporter and by White House Deputy Press Secretary Bill Burton, though the latter explained it, "We did reach out to him prior to the press conference to tell him that we had been paying attention to what he had been doing on Iran and there was a chance that he'd be called on. And, he ended up asking the toughest question that the President took on Iran. In the absence of an Iranian press corps in Washington, it was an innovative way to get a question directly from an Iranian."

7   "Bouazizi: The Man Who Set Himself and Tunisia on Fire," by Rania Abouzeid, *Time*, January 21, 2011.

8   Tunisian courts dropped the charges against the policewoman, Fedia Hamdi, on the grounds that Bouazizi's family had withdrawn their complaint.

9   "The Consequentialist: How the Arab Spring Remade Obama's Foreign Policy," by Ryan Lizza, *The New Yorker*, May 2, 2011.

10   From a White House press release on the events in Tunisia, January 14, 2011.

11   After a short stint in the US, he ended up back in Egypt. It was there that he

died, and was given a state funeral by President Anwar Sadat, on July 27, 1980.

12   The first public expression of Carter's support was on November 15, 1977, during a state visit by the Shah to Washington. Rioting erupted prior to and during the proceedings on the White House lawn, as thousands of pro- and anti-Shah Iranians residing in the US demonstrated. The police were forced to fire tear gas at the crowd. This resulted in both leaders and their wives spending the ceremony dabbing their eyes with handkerchiefs. The next day, Carter quipped: "There's one thing about that Shah: he sure knows how to draw a crowd."

But in Iran, where no such display of protest so close to a leader and his visitors could take place without the consent of the monarchy, the event was interpreted as a sign that Carter was turning his back on the Shah.

A month and a half later, on New Year's Eve, Carter paid a state visit to Iran. At a banquet held for him at Navarian Palace, Carter made a toast in which he said that "Iran, because of the great leadership of the Shah, is an island of stability in one of the more troubled areas of the world."

This would become one of Carter's more ridiculed statements, since a mere year hence, the monarchy would be toppled by the Islamic revolution.

13   He would subsequently flee to France, where he was assassinated in 1991 for his anti-Islamic Republic activities.

14   One of the Marines, 22-year-old Sgt. Kenneth Kraus, was abducted from his hospital bed in Tehran and held by Khomeini's Revolutionary Committee. Deputy Prime Minister Abbas Amir Entezami said he would be tried for "firing on Iranians." Nevertheless, he was released a week later, following negotiations between the embassy and the government. Once free, Kraus recounted that he was thrown to the floor and shot *after* surrendering.

15   This was due to their having fled Iran a result of Mossadeq's ouster. That their "Liberation of Iran" movement continued to conduct anti-Shah activities abroad did not seem to be cause for pause as to their corresponding attitude towards the US.

16   Just over nine months later, Carter would send Clark and staff director for the Senate Select Committee on Intelligence William Miller to Iran to negotiate with Khomeini for the release of the hostages held at the US Embassy. But Khomeini would refuse to meet with his staunch defender, whom he prevented from entering the country.

17   These remarks were dismissed the following day at a news briefing by White House press secretary Jody Powell. "It is President Carter's view that the United States is not in the canonization business," he stated.

Young would end up having to resign six months later, without any connection to his views on Iran, but as a result of his meeting with a PLO representative at the UN and then lying about it to the State Department. On this, Carter wrote: "Accepting the resignation of Andrew Young was one of the most heart-wrenching decisions I had to make as president. He was a close and intimate friend..." (*White House Diary*, by Jimmy Carter; Farrar, Straus, and Giroux, 2010; page 352.)

18   Arthur Herman, *Commentary*, December, 2009.

19   *Guests of the Ayatollah: The First Battle in America's War with Militant Islam*, by Mark Bowden; Atlantic Monthly Press, 2006.

20   Ibid.

21   *All Fall Down: America's Tragic Encounter with Iran*, by Gary Sick; Random House, 1986.

22   Bar Report, December/January, 1999.

23   This amounted to 13 all together. Two of the female embassy employees believed to be CIA agents were kept for the duration of the crisis.

24   This would backfire. Though these hostages read pro-revolution and anti-American statements for the media before their release, they were not taken seriously by the American public. Upon their return home, they told stories of mistreatment at the hands of the hostage-takers.

25   *White House Diary*, p. 373.

26   Less than two weeks later, the Shah would be transported to Panama, to take

up temporary residence at the home of former Panamanian ambassador to the US Gabriel Lewis.

27   This was when the senator accidentally drove his car off a bridge on Chappaquiddick Island in Massachusetts, and left his passenger, Mary Jo Kopechne, to die in the water. This he did while extricating himself from the car and swimming to safety. Because he had not been with his wife that evening, and then failed to inform police of the accident until the next day, rumors flew about the sexual nature of his relationship with Kopechne, with suggestions that the event may not have been accidental. He eventually pleaded guilty to leaving the scene of an accident after causing injury and received a suspended sentence. Though the scandal did not hurt his career in the Senate, it may have been the reason for his not running as Democratic presidential nominee in 1972 and 1976.

28   The strained US relationship with Libya would become a source of difficulty for Carter, whose brother, Billy, was being courted by the Qaddafi regime in a "People to People" initiative geared at enabling Libya to purchase arms by going through business channels, rather than official government ones. Though Billy Carter's dealings were a subject of embarrassment to the president, and would become the focus of an investigation, Jimmy Carter nevertheless tried to enlist his brother's help in trying to get Qaddafi to intervene on behalf of the hostages in Iran.

29   After the release of the hostages, the name of the show, hosted by Koppel until 2005, would become "Nightline."

30   Today, a ceramic likeness of the ribbon is attached to the same oak tree at the residence where the Laingens still live. During an interview with Laingen for the book, he took me to the yard to show it to me, while praising his wife's campaign.

31   During the raid, the commander of the elite unit that carried it out, Jonathan Netanyahu (Yoni), was killed. He is the late brother of Israeli Prime Minister Benjamin Netanyahu.

32 From *Delta Force*, by Col. Charlie A. Beckwith [Ret.]; Avon Books, 1983.

33 At the two-day meeting, which took place December 11-12, 1979, it was decided that the US would deploy more ballistic and cruise missiles in Europe, while withdrawing nuclear warheads. Vance said the purpose of this was to remain protected, while engaging in serious nuclear arms control negotiations with the Soviets.

34 Airborne Warning and Control Systems, installed in planes to monitor air traffic in the vicinity.

35 *White House Diary*, entry from December 9, 1979.

36 Ibid.

37 Ibid.

38 *Guests of the Ayatollah.*

39 From Coffin's obituary in *The Telegraph*, April 14, 2006.

40 *Guests of the Ayatollah.*

41 *Yellow Ribbon: The Secret Journal of Bruce Laingen;* Brassey's Inc., 1992.

42 Ibid.

43 Excerpted from the text of "The President's News Conference," February 8, 1977.

44 *White House Diary*, February 14, 1977.

45 *Time*, June 25, 1979. ("'Korosho,' Said Brezhnev.")

46 *The Present Danger*, by Norman Podhoretz; Simon and Schuster, 1980.

47 *White House Diary*, part of June 18, 1979 entry.

48 *All Fall Down*, by Gary Sick.

49 *White House Diary*, entry from December 28, 1979.

50 *White House Diary*, entry from December 31, 1979.

51 Parts of this film, in which the hostages are reading anti-American statements on camera, while wishing "Imam Khomeini" a merry Christmas, were also broadcast on stations, much to the horror of the American public.

52 *Yellow Ribbon*, entry from January 1, 1980.

53 Though Carter did recall Ambassador Thomas Watson "for consultations" on

January 2, he sent him back to the Soviet Union on January 18. This caused a commotion among Pan Am crew at Kennedy Airport, who refused to service the Aeroflot carrier on which he flew to Moscow.

54   *White House Diary*, entry from January 2, 1980.

55   Ibid, entry from January 14.

56   One of the hostages managed to get an uncensored letter past his captors, and sent to the White House—probably through the aid of a foreign worker among the kitchen staff.

57   *White House Diary*, entry from January 22, 1980.

58   *The Present Danger.*

59   American-Canadian relations were on an all-time high after this. Upon his return from Tehran, Ambassador Taylor was appointed Canadian Consul-General to New York City. Because of his heroic role in the "caper," he was made an Officer of the Order of Canada and was awarded the United States Congressional Gold Medal.

60   *White House Diary*, entry from February 7, 1980.

61   Khomeini instated Bani-Sadr as president of the Islamic Republic in a ceremony from his hospital bed—where he was being treated for a heart ailment—on February 4.

62   "U.N. Putting Off Trade Sanctions against Teheran," by Bernard Gwertzman, *The New York Times*, February 7, 1980.

63   *White House Diary*, entry from February 15, 1980.

64   *All Fall Down.*

65   The commission was comprised of five members: Andrés Aguilar Mawdsley, former Venezuelan ambassador to both the UN and the US, chairman of the UN Commission on Human Rights, and president of the Inter-American Commission on Human Rights, who had headed a special team that investigated human rights violations in Nicaragua and came down hard on the Somoza regime; Mohammed Bedjaoui, Algeria's chief delegate to the UN and member of the UN International Law Commission; Adib Daoudy, foreign

affairs adviser to Syrian President Hafez Assad, who, though pro-Khomeini, thought the hostage crisis was harmful to Islam; Hector Wilfred Jayawardene, brother of Sri Lanka President Juni Richard Jayawardene, and chairman of the Sri Lanka Foundation Institute that promotes democracy and human rights; Louis-Edmond Pettiti, a Frenchman, founder of the Institute for Training in Human Rights, who once headed a team that investigated torture committed by the Shah's security forces.

66   *Associated Press*, March 11, 1980.

67   *Yellow Ribbon*, entry from February 25, 1980.

68   *White House Diary*, entry from March 25, 1980.

69   *All Fall Down*.

70   Ibid.

71   *Delta Force*.

72   Boykin, the author of *Never Surrender; a Soldier's Journey to the Crossroads of Faith and Freedom*, retired from the military in 2007, after 36 years of service. This included his command of Delta Force, then of all US Army Special Forces, a tour at the CIA and as deputy undersecretary of defense for intelligence. His comments are taken from an interview I conducted with him in his hometown of Richmond, Virginia in October, 2010.

73   "Excerpts from Iranians' Messages," *The New York Times*, April 2, 1980.

74   "Bani-Sadr Sets Terms for Hostage Shift," by John Kifner, *The New York Times*, April 2, 1980.

75   *All Fall Down*.

76   *Delta Force*.

77   *White House Diary*, entry from April 7, 1980.

78   Ayatollah Mohammad Baqir al-Sadr and his sister, Bint al-Huda, were well-known for their Islamist ideology.

79   *White House Diary*, entry from April 10, 1980.

80   *Never Surrender*.

81   *White House Diary*, entry from April 27, 1980.

82   *The New York Times*, "News Summary," May 1, 1980.

83   "Iran Dashes British Hopes for American Hostages," by John Kifner (reporting from Iran), *The New York Times*, May 7.

84   *White House Diary*, entry from May 9, 1980.

85   Though it was understood that Britain, unlike the US, had the "home turf" advantage—and that it, unlike Iran, was protecting foreign diplomats on its soil—the event nevertheless stirred awe and envy among the American public.

86   "Summary of the summary of the judgment of 24 May 1980 case concerning United States diplomatic and consular staff in Tehran," from the ICJ website.

87   He won the prize for "Physiology or Medicine," but was a vocal political activist. At a lecture at MIT in 1969 during the Vietnam War, he accused the United States of being "preoccupied with death, with the business of killing and being killed."

88   "Iran: Baiting the US," *Time* magazine, June 16, 1980.

89   "Merced, California Remarks and a Question-and-Answer Session at a Town Meeting," July 4, 1980, published by the American Presidency Project.

90   "The Shah and the Hostages," by Bernard Gwertzman, *The New York Times*, July 28, 1980.

91   *White House Diary*, entry from July 31, 1980.

92   Ibid.

93   All of the above quotes are excerpted from the full transcript of Carter's address to the Democratic National Convention on July 1, 1980, from the website of the Miller Center at the University of Virginia.

94   *White House Diary*, entry from August 4, 1980.

95   Ibid. Entry from August 24, 1980.

96   Ibid. Comments on his entry from September 17, 1980.

97   *The Real Jimmy Carter*, by Steven F. Hayward; Regnery Publishing, Inc. 2004.

98   Within months, Iran had the upper hand, preventing Saddam from realizing his goals. But the war would last for eight full years, and claim some half a million lives.

99   *Yellow Ribbon*, entry from September 22, 1980.

100   The Algeria-brokered accords were signed on January 19, 1981—the day before Ronald Reagan was inaugurated.

101   *Yellow Ribbon.*

102   Ibid. Entry from December 29, 1980.

103   That war, during which chemical weapons were reported to have been used by both sides, lasted for eight years, and ended with massive casualties and no border changes.

104   Excerpted from the full transcript of Reagan's first inaugural address.

105   "Post Withholds Anderson 'Invasion' Column," August 17, 1980.

106   *October Surprise: America's Hostages in Iran and the Election of Ronald Reagan*; Three Rivers Press, 1992.

107   The announcement that he had resigned, and that his authority was transferred to the Supreme Council of the Armed Forces, was made by Vice President Omar Suleiman.

108   This is ironic, since the military ended up siding with the protestors against Mubarak. Harassing journalists covering the demonstrations, then, made no sense.

109   This and the above quotes are from Logan's TV interview with CBS's "Sixty Minutes" on April 28, 2011—two and a half months after the assault.

110   "CBS Reporter Recounts a 'Merciless' Assault," by Brian Stelter, *The New York Times*, April 28, 2011.

111   Ibid.

112   Ibid.

113   Ibid.

114   In November, in the lead-up to the parliamentary elections, two other female journalists were sexually assaulted while doing their job. One was French television journalist Caroline Sinz. Another was Mona Eltahawy, a New York-based Egyptian-American reporter, who accused security forces of committing the acts, which left her with broken bones.

115 The Organization of the Islamic Conference (OIC) is a political-religious entity aiming to impose Sharia law on the entire Muslim world and beyond. It has close ties to the Muslim Brotherhood, and it supports jihadist movements. If Obama was unaware of this, it is not a good sign. If he was, it is even worse.

116 It is estimated that approximately 300 anti-government protesters were killed during that period—some of them at the hands of pro-Mubarak protesters, not the regime.
Other measures the regime took against the protesters included the shutting down of Internet access.

117 Excerpts from Obama's statement from February 11, 2011.

118 This was a variation on the motto of the anti-Mubarak demonstrations: "The people want to bring down the regime."

119 This was the second such attack; the first took place on February 5, a week before Mubarak's final ouster.

120 The elections would end up being postponed until November.

121 According to an Amnesty International report, these female demonstrators had not only been forced to submit to virginity tests, but had also been beaten, given electric shocks, strip-searched and threatened with prostitution charges.

122 Both ElBaradei and Nour have dubious "democratization" credentials. ElBaradei, the Nobel laureate head of the International Atomic Energy Agency for more than a decade, was a staunch apologist for Iran's nuclear program. In spite of all the emerging reports about Iran's capabilities and intentions, he remains adamant that he hadn't misled anyone. Nour, a darling of the West who had been imprisoned for four years in 2005 by the regime on trumped-up charges, showed his true colors as soon as Mubarak was ousted. Announcing his intention to run for president, he stated that the 30-year peace treaty between his country and Israel should be nullified, as it "no longer served Egypt's interests."

123 "Carter Says Egypt's Military Is Likely to Retain Some Political Powers," by David. D. Kirckpatrick, *The New York Times*, January 11, 2012.

124 "America and the Arab Spring," *The Jerusalem Post*, January 23, 2012.

125 Ibid.

126 "Foreign policy for Republicans, and others: Part I," *The Jerusalem Post*, February 10, 2012.

127 "Islam is Islam, and That's It," by Andrew C. McCarthy, National Review Online, January 23, 2012.

Acknowledgments

This book could not have been written without the help of a great number of people. First and foremost, I am grateful to David J. Azrieli, who conceived of its thesis, and whose generous grant enabled me to travel far and wide to interview figures crucial to the story.

I would like to thank David Horovitz, my former boss at *The Jerusalem Post*, for his endless guidance and support.

Many others made themselves available to me for interviews, in spite of their busy schedules. I am naming them here in alphabetical order: John Bolton, William Boykin, Richard Carlson, Yigal Carmon, Rachel Ehrenfeld, Hillel Fradkin, Lela Gilbert, Caroline B. Glick, Dore Gold, Wade Ishimoto, Henry Kissinger, Bruce Laingen, Barbara Ledeen, Michael Ledeen, Bernard Lewis, I. Lewis "Scooter" Libby, Uri Lubrani, Andrew C. McCarthy, Fiamma Nirenstein, Richard Perle, Harold Rhode, Barry Rosen, Dan Schueftan, Itzik Segev, Martin Sherman, Amir Taheri, and R. James "Jim" Woolsey, Jr.

Finally, I would like to thank my publisher, René van Praag, for his faith in the manuscript.

CPSIA information can be obtained at www.ICGtesting.com
Printed in the USA
LVOW13s0225060814

397699LV00021B/143/P